How to Make a Citizen's Arrest:
Secrets Private Investigators, Bounty Hunters and Loss Prevention Officers Know

by: Larry Kaye, P.I.

© Copyright 2015

All rights reserved.
No part of this publication may be reproduced, transmitted or recorded by any means without prior written consent of the publisher, Be Amazing Productions, LLC.

Requests for permission may be sent to:
Be Amazing Productions, LLC
3971 Hoover Road, #281
Grove City OH 43123

Legal Notice

This book is not about what's a legal. It's about what's real.

Neither the publisher nor the author is an attorney and makes no legal claims regarding the contents of this publication. Any questions of law should be directed to an attorney. While attempts have been made to verify the accuracy of the materials contained in this book, the author, the publisher and the distributor assumes no responsibility for errors, omissions, use or misuse of this material and information.

Neither the publisher nor the author is a doctor and makes no medical claims regarding the contents of this publication. Any questions of health or medicine should be directed to a licensed physician.

For purposes of ease of reading and since the English language doesn't have a gender neutral pronoun for people, the author frequently use "he" rather than "her or she". Obviously both men and women can make a citizen's arrest. Likewise both men and women can be criminals.

This book is for information purposes only.

The purchaser assumes total responsibility for the use of these materials and information.

It's your responsibility to know and follow the law. PERIOD.

ABOUT THE AUTHOR

Larry Kaye, Private Investigator and author.

Larry is considered the trusted authority in private investigator training.

After getting his Private Investigator's license, Larry owned and ran his own detective agency for nine years before semi-retiring to mostly conduct training and provide consulting services.

With thousands of hours of surveillance and investigative experience, Larry's training materials are considered "must have" by experienced investigators around the world.

Larry is a frankly-awesome skip tracer, strangely good listener, blogger and all around nice guy who knows some scary things.

He is the creator of The Investigator's Ultimate Guide Series. The series is premium Private Investigator training from someone who's been there and done that.

Larry shares his best secrets in his books and videos relying on their premium pricing to put them only in the hands of men and women interested in acting ethically when conducting their investigations.

Larry blogs at **ShadowAnyone.com** with too little self-consciousness on things that matter to him and occasionally goes completely off the deep end.

Plus he's a total Jesus Freak, so he's always got that going for him.

TABLE OF CONTENTS

Introduction 1

Understanding the Basics 3

Preparation 6

Equipment 11

Making the Decision 13

Is the Crime a Felony 18

Anatomy of an Arrest 20

Bystanders 26

The Arrest 28

Timing 32

Recording 33

How Far to Follow the Suspects 34

When to Approach the Suspect 36

Chasing the Suspect 37

Be Confident 41

"Magic" Phrases 42

Use of Force 45

Should You Use a Weapon 50

Restraints	53
Protecting Yourself Even More	57
Miranda Rights	59
Calling the Police	60
What the Suspect Says	61
When to Break the "Rules"	63
Can You Search the Suspect	64
The Police	66
When the Police Arrive	69
Do You Make a Written Statement	71
Myths	73
More About the Police	75
Do You Need and Attorney	76
Legal Liability	77
Common Mistakes	79
Conclusion	83
Appendix of State Laws	84
Also by Larry Kaye	99

INTRODUCTION

Are you a sheepdog?

What is a sheepdog?

Sometimes you may hear a person refer to himself as a sheepdog. The theory behind it goes something like this...

The world is roughly divided into two categories of people. The vast majority of people, perhaps 98%, are sheep. These are people who live their lives going to work, spending time with their families and being generally unaware of the dangers in the world.

There's nothing wrong with being a sheep. These people are good and decent, they're just not aware of the dangers around them.

A much smaller portion of the population, perhaps 2%, are wolves. These people are predators. They lie, cheat, steal and victimize the sheep.

There is a third category, much smaller than either of these others. This category is known as sheep dogs. Sheep dogs protect the sheep. If you're reading this you probably consider yourself a sheepdog... just like me.

Sheep dogs understand there are wolves out there and the dangers associated with the wolves. We have our heads up and we are aware that danger can strike at any time.

In a way, we think very much like the wolves. The key difference being, although we see potential victims and potential situations to take advantage of, we do not act upon those things. In fact, we tend to step up and help protect victims when we see bad things happening.

If you're a sheep dog (and if you're reading this you probably are), eventually you may need the skill of being able to make a citizen's arrest.

UNDERSTANDING THE BASICS

Who can make a citizen's arrest?

The laws about citizen's arrest vary from state to state. You are personally responsible to know the laws in your area. However, generally speaking, any citizen may make a citizen's arrest given the proper circumstances.

The ability of a citizen to make an arrest stems from a very long history of common law going back centuries in western civilization.

How much time should you expect the bad guys to get in jail?

Generally speaking criminals do relatively short terms in jail. If you're considering making a citizen's arrest because the person "deserves to go to jail", you probably shouldn't make the arrest. You may be surprised to learn that many criminals receive a suspended sentence or a very short sentence in jail, frequently 30 days or less. Usually much less.

On the other hand, if you make a mistake while making a citizen's arrest, *you* could easily find yourself in jail or prison. And as a decent, upright citizen, Murphy's law would suggest you're going to receive a much longer sentence and have a much rougher time serving that sentence than a person we typically think of as a criminal.

Accidental Crime

Believe it or not, you can even go to jail if you *accidentally* commit a crime!

Most of the time in order to be convicted of a crime the state has to prove "intent". This means one of the things they have to prove is that you *intended* to commit a crime. However there is a class of laws known as "strict liability laws". With strict liability laws the crime is committed when the person commits certain acts, whether or not they intended to commit a crime.

A classic example of a strict liability law is serving alcohol to an underage person. In some states if a bartender serves alcohol to an underage person, the bartender is guilty of the crime whether or not they *intended* to serve alcohol to an underage person. The bartender may be very opposed to serving minors. The bartender may be very diligent in checking identification cards to ensure the person is 21 or older. However, even the most well intentioned bartender can make a mistake. When this happens and they serve a minor, they are guilty whether they *intended* to serve a minor or not.

Even when the state must prove intent, most prosecutors would have very little trouble proving that you committed a crime if you make a mistake during a citizen's arrest.

The police and the prosecutors have many, many charges to choose from when deciding what to charge you with. They can charge you with false imprisonment, kidnapping, impersonating a law enforcement officer, disturbing the peace or any one of dozens of other charges. They can choose from a list of charges you may not even know exist.

In addition to criminal liability you may also face civil liability if you make a citizen's arrest. Even if the subject is proven guilty in a court of law or outright admits guilt by pleading guilty in court, you may still face civil liabilities (meaning you may be sued). Dealing with the subject's attorney is often more dangerous than making the arrest!

It's important to remember that even if the subject is convicted of the crime, he can still sue you.

In many states the length of time one has to file criminal charges is different than the length of time one has to begin a tort action (file a lawsuit). For example in Ohio if you're the victim of theft you have one year to file charges against the thief, but the thief has *two* years before he loses the ability to file a lawsuit against you. So if you make a citizen's arrest and the victim fails to file charges, or waits too long to file charges, the person you arrested can easily claim that he did *not* commit a crime because there's no conviction. That means you didn't arrest a criminal, but that you assaulted and kidnapped an innocent person!

PREPRATION

Long before you face a particular circumstance that requires the decision of whether or not you're going to make a citizen's arrest, you need to consider certain things. I call this the "preparation time", so if you decide to make a citizen's arrest you're better prepared.

One thing you need to consider is if you're the type of person who *can* make a citizen's arrest!

I don't mean if you're strong enough or physically capable. I'm talking about whether or not you have the intestinal fortitude to make a citizen's arrest. I've witnessed many grown men, who when push came to shove, simply could not stand up and make it happen. There's nothing wrong with this. These men have other skills and abilities, but making an arrest is not one of them.

This is nothing to be ashamed of. I firmly believe every individual, just by nature of being a human being, has immense value. However, if you *can't* make a citizen's arrest, it's best to recognize that right now and not when your knee deep into it!

The legal requirements are one thing, but first you need to have these three things...

The three things.

Three things must come together in order for a person to be able to make a citizen's arrest.

1. The person must be *able* to make a citizen's arrest.

This means that they're not only physically capable, but also that they have the *ability*... that unique skill set and knowledge of the law that allows them to make a citizen's arrest. They need to know what to do, how to do it and exactly what to say.

2. The person must be *willing* to make a citizen's arrest.

Even if a person is *able* to make a citizen's arrest, for a variety of reasons, he may be *unwilling* to make a citizen's arrest.

He may decide it's not worth the physical risk. He may decide it's not worth the legal risk. He may decide the severity of the crime does not warrant making an arrest. There are precious few good reasons to make a citizen's arrest, but many good reasons *not* to make a citizen's arrest.

I've been there. I have the *ability* to make a citizen's arrest, but there have been many times I was not *willing* to make the arrest! Why should I accept all of the risk for some relatively minor felony if no one is in danger and I can simply call the police instead of making the arrest myself?

3. There must be an *opportunity* to make a citizen's arrest.

Obviously if the circumstances do not warrant making a citizen's arrest, no arrests should be made. This may be because there is no crime, the crime does not rise to the level that warrants an arrest or one is not present at the proper time to make the arrest.

However when ability, willingness, opportunity come together, the citizen may decide it is time to take action. And that citizen may decide the proper action is to make an arrest.

How you do anything is how you do everything.

If you have a hot temper or don't care about important details or think you're the best judge and jury of most situations, you probably will make bad decisions about when and how to make a citizen's arrest.

The ethics that you live by everyday will become amplified in the heat of the moment when you're making a citizen's arrest.

CASE STUDY: A perfect example is the first time I was involved in a felony apprehension. While I personally did not make the arrest, it was a great experience for me to learn about these things and prepared me for when I eventually would begin making citizen's arrests.

I was working for a private security company as a K-9 patrol officer. The business model was that the city was divided into five sectors and each sector had a K-9 patrol officer assigned to it. The security officer drove a marked car and carried a dog with him. Businesses within the city would contract with the security company for protective services. A business could decide how often they wanted a K-9 patrol to come to their property.

One business might want a K-9 patrol to come in three times a night, but always after midnight. Another business might want a K-9 patrol to come through once every hour all night long. My job as a K-9 security officer was to patrol my section of the city, going from business to business, providing security for those businesses.

Additionally, a large part of my job was to respond to alarms at those businesses.

Early one morning, while it was still dark, just as my shift was about to end, one of the other security officers was dispatched on a power failure alarm. While this was outside of my district, it was nearby and on my way back to the garage so I radioed that I would take the alarm run.

If you have any experience with alarm response you know that essentially every time an alarm goes off it's a false alarm. And in this case it was a "power failure alarm" which seems even less urgent... even if it is a real alarm. The worst it could really be is a blown circuit breaker or perhaps a transformer in the neighborhood went out.

The way most guards approach this is to drive straight up to the building, hop out of the car, go up to the front door and look at the alarm panel. But I approached it a little bit differently.

On the dozens and dozens (and perhaps 100 plus) alarms I had been dispatched to, I always approached them as if they were real. So when I responded to this alarm I took the same actions. They were instinctual for me.

About half a block away I blacked out the patrol car (turned off all the lights), rolled down the windows and virtually coasted up to the business. I stopped on the street before entering the parking lot of the business. I looked at the building from across the street and nothing appeared out of place, but because the windows in the patrol car were down, I was able to listen carefully and I heard the crunch, crunch, crunch of broken glass been stepped on.

As I looked more carefully I could see one full size, ceiling to floor plate glass window had been broken out. Because it was broken out completely and because it didn't have any broken glass pieces hanging from the edges, it was initially difficult to see that it was missing. The habit of approaching properly and listening carefully, changed everything about this "power failure" alarm.

I radioed in that I had a burglary in progress and the police were dispatched. I watched as the burglar carried armload after armload of computer equipment out of the building and hid it. The burglar finally had taken all that he wanted and began to walk away through a park intending to come back later to retrieve the computer equipment he had hidden nearby.

By time the police pulled up he was already gone, but I had followed and kept an eye on him. I flagged down the officers as they arrived. After the first officers arrived and realized they had an actual felony in progress, they radioed in and half a dozen police cars responded.

The police were quickly able to take him into custody.

The point of this case study is: How you do anything is how you do everything. If I had responded sloppily to "another stupid false alarm", I would've walked right into a burglary in progress and the outcome would have been very different.

If you're considering that you may have to make a citizen's arrest someday, *now* is the time to start behaving professionally about this type of thing.

EQUIPMENT

You don't need to carry any special equipment with you "just in case" you have to make a citizen's arrest.

There's no need to carry handcuffs or zip ties or any other special items on a day-to-day basis. If you can't handle a citizen's arrest in the moment, with what you have with you, you probably should not be making the arrest.

This isn't a case study of a citizen's arrest, but it makes a good point...

One winter after a heavy snowfall, I watched a snowplow operator with a great, new truck and plow plowing a parking lot. Even though I'm not in that business, I could tell the gear he had would make anyone who did that for a living envious. However, he was doing a terrible job of plowing snow! His piles of snow were blocking parking spaces and entryways. He did not have any of the trucks lights on and wasn't even using his turn signals. He was moving in and out of the parking lot and onto the street causing confusion for drivers and creating a hazardous condition.

The point is, this guy had the greatest equipment anyone could hope for and still was unable to do the job properly! The same is true for making a citizen's arrest. You can carry handcuffs and mace and anything else you think might help you make an arrest but if you don't know how to use the equipment it's only going to get you into trouble. And even if you *do* know how to use the equipment, it might reflect poorly on you in the future... maybe even at a trial.

Your best asset is your brain, everything else is just a tool.

While I've never had to use any mixed martial arts skills to make a citizen's arrest, I am a strong believer in having a handful of moves in which you are well practiced and well versed in using. The primary reason for this is because it will increase your *confidence* which is perhaps the single most important (intangible) thing when making a citizen's arrest.

MAKING THE DECISION

What are you gonna get out of it?

A key question to ask yourself in preparation for possibly making a citizen's arrest someday is, "What am I gonna get out of it?"

If you're going to make a citizen's arrest for any reason other than to protect a victim you're probably doing it for the wrong reason.

Maybe you're a private investigator and you think this could be good publicity for you and your agency. You've got to ask yourself, "Is it worth it?"

There are a lot better ways to get publicity than by making a citizen's arrest. Getting the arrest *wrong* can cost you everything. You can be sued or imprisoned.

Also you have to remember how easily and commonly things are video recorded. Do you really want what you're about to do posted online forever?

The news story headline could easily read: Local Private Investigator Charged with Impersonating a Law Enforcement Officer. Likewise you could be charged with kidnapping, false imprisonment, wrongful arrest, breach of peace or just about any one of a million other charges!

The laws on when a citizen can make an arrest vary from state to state. You, and only you, are responsible to know and follow those laws. It bears repeating that this book is *not* designed to teach you what is legal, but to teach you what happens in the real world. I am not encouraging you to ever make a citizen's arrest. However, if one day you decide there's no other option, I want you to do it as safely as possible.

When the moment comes that you need to decide whether or not to make a citizen's arrest you need to understand the consequences.

Considering the issues in the previous chapter on preparation is a good starting place for deciding whether or not you should make a citizen's arrest.

One key piece of business advice I give to private investigators who run their own detective agencies, is to say "no" more often. By that I mean, when potential clients contact you, hoping to hire you to work their case, there will be many, many times the smartest thing you can say to the potential client is "no". You may be tempted to take the case because you need the money, but those are precisely the cases that tend to be the most expensive and most troublesome. In fact, some of those cases you would gladly *pay* to get rid of. It's valuable to remember that when you're deciding whether or not to make a citizen's arrest.

My basic rule of thumb is: Leave it to the pros. Let the police make the arrest.

If you're witnessing a crime in progress, remember *recording* the crime is almost as good as making an arrest!

MYTH: A common piece of advise I see given...

You may have heard that you should never make an arrest unless you have a partner or witness with you. Many so-called "experts" will tell you not to attempt to make an arrest by yourself. And while this is excellent advice, the reality is, most of the time if an arrest needs to be made, you're the only person willing to step up and take care of business. Interestingly, when you begin to take action the people around you may begin to get "braver". Hopefully if you find yourself making an arrest you won't be alone. At the very least it's nice to have someone who will record the arrest for you. This can be an excellent piece of protection for you if something goes wrong.

I've never had video "jam me up", but there have been many times when video has saved to me! After the fact, anyone reviewing the video can see that I acted reasonably regardless of the bias of witnesses or the false claims of people who were involved.

When is a crime occurring?

Sometimes it's not always obvious when a crime is occurring. Many times a crime in progress doesn't look like it does on television or in the movies. On a day-to-day basis it can be helpful to look not only for what's "wrong", but in any given circumstance also look for what's *different*.

CASE STUDY: One time when I was working as a loss prevention officer, I saw a man coming out of a neighboring retail store. He was pushing a shopping cart with a large box on top of it. The box was a computer and monitor. This was back when monitors were the old, large Cathode Ray Tube monitors. This was not a small thing.

I was doing parking lot surveillance and I'm not sure why the man caught my eye, but I noticed he was pushing the cart far out into the parking lot. He pushed the cart into another businesses' parking lot (which was odd), where he met a driver who opened up the hatchback of the waiting car. They placed the computer in the back of the car, almost tossing it in the back, rather than gently placing it like a new computer owner would do.

Also it struck me as odd that the driver didn't come up to meet the man as he came out of the store. So I drove over and wrote down their license plate number as they left the property.

I went into the neighboring store, and while there were six or seven employees within 50 feet of the front door (and none of them were helping customers), I still couldn't get their attention.

Finally I pulled out my badge and ask to speak to a manager. They quickly got the manager and I told him I thought someone just stole a computer from his store. I described what I saw being pushed out on top of the shopping cart (it was too large to fit inside the shopping cart). The manager and I quickly went down the aisle where the computers were stocked and saw a large open space were one had been taken.

The man had simply loaded the computer onto the shopping cart and pushed it out of the store. This store was set up so the only way out was through a checkout lane. Which means he moved with confidence and the employees ignored him, just that as they had ignored me when I had walked in.

The manager called the police and an officer was dispatched to take a report.

When the uniformed officer arrived he was surprised to hear what had happened. He said he thought an undercover police officer was working in the parking lot because of the busy Christmas season. He said he would have expected the plain clothes officer to have radioed in anything suspicious.

The responding officer got on a radio back-channel and raised the undercover officer. The uniformed officer, who was taking the report, explained that there was a theft. The only thing the undercover officer could say was, "I didn't see anyone running through the parking lot or anything like that."

What I had noticed was not necessarily "criminal activity" like the plain clothes officer was looking for, but behavior that was *out of the ordinary*. Normally a waiting driver comes up to greet a customer with a large load as he comes out of a store. What I noticed was something "different".

The point of this case study is you're not always looking for what's "wrong". Sometimes you're looking for what's *different*. In this case I recognized the crime of theft because I noticed, not what was wrong, but what was different.

Look for what's different.

IS THE CRIME A FELONY?

One of the most important elements when deciding whether or not to make a citizen's arrest is deciding whether or not the crime is a felony.

Crimes are generally divided into two categories felonies and misdemeanors.

Felonies are more serious crimes usually punishable by one year or more in prison. Common examples are murder, rape and kidnapping.

Misdemeanors are less serious crimes usually punishable by less than one year in the county jail. Common examples include petty theft, public intoxication and disturbing the peace.

It's important to determine if the crime is a felony because in many states one of the requirements for a citizen's arrest is that the crime be a felony. Generally speaking, private citizens are *not* authorized to make misdemeanor arrest.

Sometimes it's difficult to tell if a crime is a felony or misdemeanor. For example the theft of less than $1000 may be a misdemeanor, while the same exact same theft of $1000 or more may be a felony. The crime will look *exactly* the same to an outside observer, but it's the dollar amount that determines whether or not a felony is involved.

It's important to remember, just because you know that a crime is a felony or a misdemeanor, that doesn't mean it will *always* be that way. State legislatures routinely change the dollar value required for crime to become a felony. At one time a theft of $300 or more was a felony in the state of Ohio. If you make a citizen's arrest for a theft because you know the value of the stolen item is $400 and you believe that makes it a felony, you would be dead *wrong* because the law has changed and (at the time of this writing) *$1,000* is the felony amount in Ohio!

Likewise sometimes crimes are *reclassified* from felonies to misdemeanors by a state's legislature. Sometimes this is done to make crime statistics look lower from one year to the next and sometimes it's done to relieve overcrowded prisons. For example, if possession of an ounce of marijuana is a felony, the state legislature might reduce that particular crime to a misdemeanor so when a conviction is made the person is more likely to go to a county jail rather than a state prison.

The key element here is that you need to be up to date on what is a felony in your state.

Some states do allow a private citizen to make an arrest for certain misdemeanors such as breach of peace. Although it varies from state to state, breach of peace offenses are generally things like brawling, public intoxication, batteries, riots, forcible entry or perhaps discharging a restricted weapon. I personally cannot imagine why anyone would make a citizen's arrest for a misdemeanor of that nature. This next point is also extremely important...

Many times you may see what you *think* looks like a crime but it's completely legitimate and legal. In many states openly carrying a firearm is a legal activity. If you see someone carrying a firearm legally and you mistakenly think it's a crime, it will *not* end well for you.

Some states allow specific private citizens authorization to make a misdemeanor arrest under specific circumstances. For example, in Ohio a store detective or loss prevention officer is acting as an "agent of the merchant" and an agent of the merchant is specifically (by statute) authorized to make misdemeanor arrest for items stolen from the store. This was one of my earliest jobs in private security and I loved it. It was a fun job where I was able to gain experience apprehending or "arresting" hundreds and hundreds of thieves.

ANATOMY OF AN ARREST

Hearsay

Part of determining if the crime is a felony is based on what you personally witness and what you might hear from others. While "hearsay" is generally not admissible in a court of law, there are exceptions and in the context of a crime in progress or crime that's just been completed, part of what you'll be basing your decision on may be what people tell you.

If you see people excitedly pointing and saying, "That's him! That's him!" at a man who's running away, that's part of what you're going to take into consideration in determining if a crime is being committed and if it's a felony. And while that particular example may not be enough for a legitimate arrest, it's one factor that you'll have to consider.

I regret that I even have to say this, but...

WARNING: Don't make an arrest if a crime has not happened!

Reasonable Suspicion

The first point of determining if a crime has been committed is "reasonable suspicion". A reasonable suspicion is a general and reasonable belief that a crime is in progress or has occurred. If you don't have a reasonable belief or a reasonable suspicion that a crime has occurred, then you lack the most basic element for making a citizen's arrest.

Probable Cause

In addition to reasonable suspicion you also have to have "probable cause" to make a citizen's arrest. Probable cause is a set of facts and circumstances that would induce a reasonably intelligent and prudent person to believe that a particular other person has committed a specific crime.

CASE STUDY: Once when I was in a drugstore I saw a pharmacist, in her white lab coat, run out the front door and my initial thought was she was chasing a shoplifter. However, I could tell by her manner, bearing and urgency that, whatever it was, it was something serious.

I caught up with a pharmacist, flashed my P.I. badge and asked if there was anything I could do to help. The pharmacist pointed to a young woman running across the parking lot and said, "Stop her!"

I caught up with the young woman and stopped her without having to use physical force. When the pharmacist caught up to us she told me the young woman presented a fraudulent prescription and attempted to get narcotics. I escorted the young woman back into the drug store and waited until the police arrived.

In this particular case I had not *witnessed* a felony, but based on the pharmacist's actions and her mannerisms, I had reason to believe a felony had been committed. (Notice I had "reasonable belief".) Most large stores have a policy prohibiting employees from chasing shoplifters so I quickly figured whatever the problem was it had to be pretty significant. In this case it was attempting to obtain narcotics with a fraudulent prescription, which in my state is a felony.

Because the pharmacist seemed like a credible source of information and because she was the actual victim identifying the criminal, I had probable cause to believe the young woman who was running away from the scene was the individual who committed the crime. (Notice I had "probable cause".)

You may never *have* to articulate your reasonable belief and probable cause, however you should *understand* this very well before you ever attempt a citizen's arrest.

While I've made about half a dozen citizen's arrests not related to any job or occupation I had, I've *passed up* many more opportunities, deciding the circumstances weren't right for me to make an arrest. Almost always my bottom line question when determining whether to make an arrest is, "Is someone in danger?" If no one's in danger, if it's not a crime of violence, there's frequently no reason (in my view) to make an arrest.

I highly recommend that you be *reluctant* to make an arrest.

HUGE TIP: In most circumstances you can contribute more than enough by simply observing and reporting.

If you get the full and accurate license plate number of someone fleeing the scene of a crime, I can almost promise that you'll be the only witness who does! Unprepared an untrained witnesses are notorious for reporting incomplete and incorrect information. And while sometimes criminals will use a stolen car or stolen license plates, most of the time the license plate information you collect will be extremely valuable to the police and contribute directly to the apprehension and conviction of the criminal.

Additionally, if you're *not* making the arrest, you're free to call the police. Believe me, they will be greatly appreciative of a calm, observant witness who can report over the phone the information they need. An accurate description of the subject(s), vehicle, license plate number and/or direction of travel may very well make the difference between an arrest and a clean getaway for the bad guy.

Suspect Description

One thing that many so-called experts teach about getting a suspect's description is that you should ignore things that can be easily changed... such as shoes. While shoes can be easily changed, many people wear the same shoes for days and weeks on end. And certainly within the minutes or even hours after crime is committed, and especially while a suspect is still fleeing, an accurate description of the suspect (including the shoes he's wearing!) can make a world of difference. If this seems odd to you, I can assure you after years and years of working in the field, this can mean the difference between a successful arrest and no arrests at all.

At this point in your decision-making process (whether or not to make a particular arrest), I want you to presume that you are being video recorded. So ask yourself if what you're about to do something that you want posted online *forever*. If this thought makes you hesitate, you should definitely reconsider making the arrest.

The Suspect

The next thing you have to figure out is if this is the right guy!

Is the person you're considering arresting *truly* the person who committed the crime? Maybe he's a scared witness fleeing the area or perhaps even the victim. If you make a citizen's arrest and discover you've arrested the *wrong* person, the consequences for you are dire.

You must be able to articulate your probable cause for arresting *this particular person*.

How may suspects are involved?

You also have to consider if the suspect is alone or if there are others involved. Depending on the crime, my experience is about half the time there is someone else with a bad guy. It may be "only" a getaway driver or even just a friend who didn't even know about the crime, but when you go to make an arrest you may find yourself with more than one bad guy to deal with. A bad guy's friend will turn into the bad guy's aggressive ally if he believes you are hurting his friend.

Is the suspect armed?

Consider also if the bad guy (or one of his friends) might be armed. This can dramatically change your decision to make an arrest.

Whether or not he's armed, you have to think about who may get hurt if you make this arrest.

Obviously *you* may get hurt and you may be willing to accept that risk, but you also have to take into consideration what happens if the *bad guy* gets hurt while you're arresting him! When you arrest someone you're accepting responsibility for what happens to him. You also have to consider if *others* around you might get hurt.

CASE STUDY: One time, as a loss prevention officer, I was making an arrest of a couple of shoplifters, a man and a woman. I was working alone and by time I'd caught up to them they had made it to their van. I knew the police were called and we're going arrive so if I couldn't actually make the arrest, at least I could slow down the bad guys until the police arrived. At one point I jumped into the back of the van attempting to apprehend the man (or at lease slow him down). The woman began shouting to him, "Should I get the gun? Should I get the gun?"

I could tell they were going to be able to drive off so I hopped out of the van. I had every opportunity to slash one of the van's tires to slow them down or prevent them from fleeing. However, my concern was, if they were unable to escape in the van and they had a gun, what would happen if they began shooting while attempting to flee on foot. I wasn't particularly worried for my safety, but I was concerned that an innocent bystander in the parking lot might get shot. So I opted not to slash the tire and let them leave.

Combining the video from the surveillance system within the store with a good license plate number I got in the parking lot, I swore out warrants for their arrest. Eventually they were picked up on unrelated charges and plead guilty to the charges that I had filed against them.

There are several lessons you can take away from that case study including that you *don't* have too physically detain someone to get justice. Also the practiced skill of getting license plate numbers under stress paid off. Of all the people around, I was the only one who thought to get a license plate number and arguably I was *more busy* and than anyone else who had the opportunity!

BONUS TIP: You can use your cell phone camera to take a picture of their license plate.

Finally, don't make the arrest if you can easily call the police. Why not let the professionals handle it? They have the manpower, the resources and the protection from civil liability that make them the perfect choice if they're available.

BYSTANDERS

When you make a citizen's arrest, there will probably be people around. And nothing draws a crowd faster than a crowd. By that I mean... when people start noticing others watching what you're doing, more people will stop to see what's going on.

Most people will simply watch or maybe make video recordings on their phones.

But there are two other types of people and they will yell at you.

Agitators

Usually after the crime has been committed, and while you're detaining the suspect, an agitator (who has no idea what crime occurred) will start running his mouth about how the person you have in custody has rights. The agitator will continue on, perhaps telling the suspect he doesn't need to stay there or complaining loudly about the actions you're taking.

"Helpers"

"Helpers" are people who have no real idea of what's going on, but they're trying to "help" you by explaining the way they think you *should* be doing things.

These helpers may be complaining that you don't have the a right to touch the person. Or they might complain that you need to read them their rights.

Helpers are like most citizens meaning they have no idea how or when to make a citizen's arrest. And while they think they're helping by "teaching" you what they think is correct, they are really only making things worse.

In my experience, neither agitators nor helpers know what they are talking about. They simply spew out things that seem to be common sense to them, without knowing a thing about the law or your right to make a citizen's arrest within the bounds of the law.

HUGE TIP: With both agitators and helpers, the key is *not* to get drawn in to their arguments. You may choose to acknowledge them, but there is *nothing* you can say or do that will convince them that they are wrong. You will *never*, ever win an argument with them or explain to them how wrong they are in the heat of this moment.

The only thing that will happen if you choose to debate with them is that you will become agitated. And when the police arrive you will seem like just as much of a nutcase as they are!

WARNING: Don't get sucked into a debate with bystanders.

Remember... you are probably are being video recorded and you should remain calm and as polite as possible. When all is said and done, you want to appear as the calm reasonable person. This will save you a *ton* of heartache down the road.

THE ARREST

MYTH: There's a myth that when you place someone under citizen's arrest you have to say clearly (and so they understand), "You are under arrest." This is a legal requirement in some areas, but also this is something that's taught by people who have never actually made a citizen's arrest.

You don't *always* have to say, "You're under arrest."

In fact, looking at California law, you are not required to "formally" arrest the suspect if, under the circumstances, a reasonable person in the suspect's position would have known he was under arrest. An example of this is if you hold the suspect by the arm and tell him you're calling the police.

One specific example in California is People v. Garcia (1969) 274 Cal. App.2d 100, 105 ["When Edwards took defendant by the arm and told him he was going to call the police he effected a citizen's arrest"].

In Johanson v. DMV (1995), the court ruled that, while the citizen making the arrest did not utter the 'magic words,' the substance of his actions constituted a valid citizens arrest.

WARNING: These are example from California and their legal value elsewhere is questionable. However some other states have similar precedents. Remember... *You* are responsible to know the law in your area and this book is not the place to learn the details of ever-changing state laws.

Maybe, just *maybe*, you might want to say "your under arrest" if you're using physical force to detain someone, but even then I'm not sure it's truly necessary. However, if you *don't* say it, the suspect will later claim he thought you were just trying to mug him and was fighting for his personal protection. Of course even if you *do* say "your under arrest", the bad guy can still say the same thing.

My experience working as a loss prevention officer is even when I properly identified myself and displayed my badge, some people (even with stolen merchandise stuffed in their pants!), will still claim they thought I was just trying to mug them. It's ludicrous, but it's one of those things you'll hear.

My opinion is, if possible, you do not want to use the phrase "citizen's arrest" or "You're under arrest." In my experience, with hundreds of apprehensions as a loss prevention officer and my experience with about half a dozen citizen's arrest not related to any job I had, I have never told the person that they are under arrest.

I think the word "arrest" or "citizen's arrest" opens up an almost knee jerk reaction to the accusation of "false arrest". I can only say that I've never used the word "arrest" and I've never been accused of false arrest.

I've also heard the advice that you should tell the suspect specifically *why* you are detaining them. I'm not sure this is always a good idea.

When I worked as a loss prevention officer being able to specifically tell the person *exactly* what they had stolen and *where* they had it concealed was an excellent tool to reduce the resistance of the shoplifter to the apprehension. When you're very specific they know you're not just guessing and their odds of bluffing their way out of it are greatly decreased. Most of the time this will cause them to give up immediately.

CASE STUDY: One time, when I was working as a loss prevention officer, a man put on a pair the store's blue jeans under the blue jeans he was wearing and walked out of the store without paying for them. He was with two women and I was working alone. By time I caught up with him he was already in the back seat of a car and the women were climbing into the front seats. I verbally identified myself showing him my badge. He immediately said,"No hablo inglés."

In terribly broken Spanish I told him he had two pairs of blue pants and one of them was mine. He let out a deep breath as his head dropped and he immediately gave up, climbing out of the car and peacefully coming back into the store with me. Being very specific can resolve some situations.

However...

I have never been specific with the people I've arrested when I've been out just living life and minding my own business. In every case like that, the mere fact that I caught up with the person seem to make them realize the situation was hopeless. And I've never had to explain in detail why I was stopping them. As soon as I caught up to them, they resigned to the inevitable and followed my verbal instructions.

I think this is because there is a part of human nature, that when caught committing a crime, a "reasonable person" (California's language) understands they are under arrest. Of course, not every bad guy just gives up when you catch him!

Experience

If you have loss prevention experience, that is a considerable asset when making a citizen's arrest out in the "real world", but there is one big difference. When you're working loss prevention making apprehensions, the bad guys are "in *your* house" so to speak. When you're out on the streets making a citizen's arrest, now you're "in *their* house". And it makes a world of difference.

A tip for today.

One thing you can start doing today that will greatly enhance your ability to make a citizen's arrest should the circumstance arise, is to practice keeping your strong hand free. By that I mean if you're right handed don't carry your briefcase or groceries or boxes in your right hand. Make sure your right hand, your dominant hand (you're strong hand) is always empty. This means your hand will be free for striking, blocking or attacking. This is a good habit to get into.

The way I was trained is the only thing that should be in your strong hand are your car keys (briefly) or your pen or pencil while you're using it.

TIMING

The timing of the arrest is very important. If you must make a citizen's arrest you want to do it during (or just after) the crime. If you see a person and know that they robbed a bank last week, do *not* make a citizen's arrest. Call the police. If you see someone on the "most wanted" list, do not make a citizen's arrest. Call the police.

It's important that your arrest occur during or just after the crime. If not, it's very likely your arrest will not be legal.

RECORDING

If you're able to record your citizen's arrest, I would suggest you begin recording as soon as possible. You don't necessarily have to hold the camera up and point it at the bad guy. Even though you might only get the audio recorded, having the camera rolling and at your side is better than nothing.

Having the arrest recorded will help you for a few reasons. First of all, because you know you're being recorded you're more likely to be reasonable and this will reflect well upon you after the arrest. Secondly, if the subject makes any incriminating remarks, this can be extremely valuable evidence to help prove you're acting lawfully. Third, having the arrest recorded helps to protect you against false accusations later. If the bad guy claims you hit him or used a racial slur or whatever, there's a good chance the recording will prove otherwise.

A recording (video or audio) of the arrest isn't guaranteed to prevent false accusations, but it may very well save your butt (as it has mine again and again!).

Of course the flip side of this is true as well. If you act unreasonably or even commit a crime while recording, you're stuck with it. Deleting the recording can lead to being charged with destruction of evidence or tampering with evidence. If you hadn't thought about that already, this should lead you to realize there are serious consequences to making a citizen's arrest, many of which you may not learn about until the prosecuting attorney finds some creative charge to stick you with.

Remember: You may not need to *physically* make the arrest. Discreetly following the suspect and keeping him in sight while you call the police will likely be enough.

HOW FAR TO FOLLOW THE SUSPECT

So how far do you follow the suspect?

One of the first considerations you need to make is whether or not the suspect is setting you up. Is he luring you to a place where he can cause you physical harm? When you decide to "hunt humans", things can very quickly turn around to where you become the hunted!

Following in a vehicle.

If you're following in a car, make sure you have enough gas. Also make sure you can drive safely while talking to the police and watching a suspect. It is very, very easy to get tunnel vision when following a bad guy. This tunnel vision can cause you to run a red light, miss a stop sign or even sideswipe another vehicle.

Also remember, just because you're the "good guy", following the criminal "for the police" doesn't mean you can break the law. It won't be a victory for you to have the police show up and take your suspect into custody only to have them turn around and arrest you for "Reckless Operation of a Motor Vehicle"! When following a suspect you are still obligated to follow all laws, just as you are *anytime* you're making a citizen's arrest.

WARNING: Another consideration when you're following a suspect in a vehicle is if *he* gets into an accident he may claim he was fearful of you and was trying to reach safety. Again this is a ridiculous claim, but you may still be held liable for the accident he causes!

Following on foot.

If you're following on foot, be especially aware if there's anyone behind you. Again you may find yourself getting in way deeper than you expected and not even realize it.

WARNING: It's also important to remember, if your suspect fleas on foot into traffic, you are responsible for any accidents or injuries that happen! Even something as "little" as a fender bender caused by a car stopping as the suspect runs across the street can cost you thousands of dollars! Is making the arrest really worth it? What if there's an accident and someone is seriously injured? You must consider these things.

This is an important point and I'm going to repeat it... Many times discreetly following the suspect and keeping him in sight while you call the police will be all you need to do and you won't have to make a citizen's arrest.

WHEN TO APPROACH THE SUSPECT

Many times when a felony is committed and you intend to make a citizen's arrest you will be at a considerable distance from the suspect. The people who are near the suspect are usually the victims and have little opportunity to do any more than comply with the criminal's demands. And perhaps that's the way it should be for the safety of everyone involved.

Since you'll frequently start out at somewhat of a distance from the suspect, you have to consider when and how to approach to suspect.

CHASING THE SUSPECT

It's generally a bad idea to chase a suspect, but if you decide to do it, here's what usually happens...

Almost every time a suspect is chased on foot the chaser is following directly behind the suspect and running in between the same cars the suspect runs between and through the same doorways. It's exactly like watching a wildlife special on television. The cheetah runs directly behind a gazelle, zigging and zagging exactly as the gazelle does, trying hard to catch up. But in the real world of catching *humans*, it's possible to *anticipate* where the suspect is going.

If the suspect is fleeing on foot, you may see that he's heading towards a hole in the fence and while he may not be taking the most direct route, if you know he has to go through the fence to get away, you may be better off running directly to the hole knowing that he's got to make it there and blocking his escape.

I've had a great deal of luck catching bad guys who are running to a getaway car by *not* chasing the bad guy, but running *directly to their car* and getting there first. I've used this tactic on a number of occasions and it works very well. In the worst case scenario they abandon the getaway car and flee on foot. In that case I still find myself with an advantage because now we're both on foot and that evens the playing field.

Call out, "Stop!"

One tactic for stopping a suspect whose fleeing on foot, and this may sound ridiculous if you've never done it, is calling out, "Stop!"

It may seem crazy that simply commanding the person to stop will make him stop, but it actually works sometimes. My theory on why this works is because in those moments of chaos the suspect's brain is trying to figure out what to do and the first and only command it receives is to "stop". This is similar to an "instant induction" used by stage hypnotist. (See: www.EasyStageHypnosis.com)

CASE STUDY: The first time I used this "Stop Command" I was shocked that my suspect stopped! He instantly gave up and I handcuffed him. The first thing he said was, " I don't know why I stopped. I was away free." And he really was! He had quite a lead on me and I doubt I would have caught him on foot. A short time later he changed his story and said he gave up because he knew it was the right thing to do. But he and I both know he stopped and he couldn't explain why. It was like magic!

Another tactic to stop the suspect.

There is another tactic you can use to stop a fleeing suspect. It's much more dangerous, but it's worked well for me in the past. The tactic is to force the suspect into making a choice between committing a more serious offense against you in order to flee or deciding just to give up because it's not worth it.

CASE STUDY: I was out one day with my buddy and as we pulled into the parking lot of a big box retailer we saw two women (one was carrying an infant) and a man running from the store. One of the store employees came running out the front door chasing after them. At this point you should understand that observing this gave me a reasonable suspicion that a crime was being committed. Additionally because most stores prohibit employees from chasing people, I could reasonably presume this was a serious crime (maybe even a felony). And because the employee was chasing these specific people, I had probable cause to believe they were the ones who committed the crime.

My buddy pulled up and blocked their car from the front, although they could still *back out* and drive away. The three very quickly made it to the car. I hopped out of my buddy's car and went immediately to the driver's side door of the suspect's vehicle. As the man came around the car to get in the driver's side, I blocked his access to the car. You'll notice in this case study I didn't have to actually chase the guy. I could tell what car they were running to so I went straight to the car and blocked the driver's door.

The man was significantly bigger than me and could have squashed me like a bug. He told me to get out of his way. I calmly asked them, "You wanna' do a felony?" He said "No." and I said, "Well you're gonna' I have to do a felony on me to get into this car."

He realized instantly this was not to his advantage. I think his reasoning was that it was unlikely the store could prove that he had done anything wrong (and that was probably true). After all (as we would find out later) he was only the "lookout" and getaway driver. Both of those roles would be difficult to prove in a court of law. He could make the defense that he didn't know what was going on and rely on the fact that the prosecution would have difficulty proving otherwise.

So in the moment, he decided, rather than to commit a provable felony on me in front of witnesses so he could get away, he would rely on the fact that it would be nearly impossible to prove beyond a reasonable doubt that he knew what the women were doing. And I think this was probably good judgment considering what the employee would explain to us next.

The employee said that the three of them were stealing and that the police had been called.

As a side note, *never* take it for granted that the police have actually been called unless you see and hear someone on the phone nearby actually talking to the police. And even then make sure they are talking to the police!

Once the police arrived, it quickly became obvious how the three were committing theft. The woman carrying the infant had a key to release the security cases attached to items they were stealing from the store. The second woman would remove the security cases, dropping them on the floor, and place the stolen merchandise in the infant's diaper bag. All three would walk out with the man at a distance acting as the lookout and getaway driver. Apparently they were stealing from this large retailer all over the city, but the only reason the retailer knew about it was because they would find piles of the empty security devices on the floor and the merchandise was missing.

When the police opened up the trunk of the car, we discovered it was full, and I mean quite full, of stolen music compact discs!

This case study has excellent examples of reasonable belief, probable cause and detaining a large suspect without using physical force. It's also an excellent example of what may be the single most important (intangible) thing when you're making a citizen's arrest... Be Confident!

BE CONFIDENT

You need to be confident and project that confidence. If you can't do that, then you probably shouldn't be making the arrest.

Being confident and projecting confidence are elements of knowing *what* to say and *how* to say it.

While it is vitally important that you *never* identify yourself as a law enforcement officer, there are certain things you can say, and need to be said, that will telegraph to the suspect that you know what you're doing and you've done this before.

The moment it becomes clear that you're there to hold the suspect accountable for his actions, you can use the following phrases to demonstrate that you know what you're doing. These phrases are so effective I call them "magic phrases".

MAGIC PHRASES

Part of the reason the suspects I've arrested didn't try to use force to get away may very well be that I took command of the situation with confidence using my "magic phrases" that indicate I have experience and proficiency in what I'm doing.

1. "Let me see your hands."

I usually say this as I'm approaching the person and well outside arm's reach. I say this for two reasons. First, in a situation like this, safety is essentially all about their hands. If you can see their hands you have a tremendous advantage. Suspects will reach into their pockets for a variety of reasons most of which are harmless like getting a cigarette. However, in order to retrieve a weapon their hands must leave your view and if you understand this it gives you a great heads up.

While you're waiting for the police the suspect may put his hand in his pocket. When that happens I simply say, "Hands". Usually the suspect simply wasn't thinking and stuck his hand into his pocket out of habit. However a quick and firm, but *calm* reminder is all it takes. This also has the added benefit of demonstrating to the suspect your proficiency at making an arrest and this apparent proficiency leads them to believe you've done this many times before.

2. "Do you have any ID on you?"

This is the type of question that is usually only asked by a police officer. And bad guys have experienced it many times before. They know it doesn't necessarily indicate an arrest and they feel like they can still talk themselves out of whatever is going on. And while you're *not* identifying yourself as a police officer, you are again demonstrating that you know what your doing.

Sometimes they will tell you they have identification and they'll reach for it. Be especially careful at this moment because, while in my experience they are genuinely getting their identification, it's the perfect opportunity for them to reach for a weapon (and experienced bad guys know this).

At least half the time the suspect will tell you he does not have identification even if he does. This is not a problem for you. The suspect knows from previous experience that even without identification he is still going to be checked out. Frequently what he's hoping is, even though he has at an active warrant out for his arrest on an unrelated charge, that you don't know about. He's thinking he can talk himself out of being arrested on *that* warrant by presenting himself as someone else, perhaps his brother or a friend. But the point is, you have demonstrated your proficiency and you've begun to take him by "baby steps" to the realization that he's not getting away.

I cannot overemphasize how these two magic phrases make a citizen's arrest go so much more smoothly and safely.

A "softer" approach.

Sometimes the suspect doesn't realize I'm detaining him (or maybe just distracting him) until the police arrive.

If it's not immediately obvious to the suspect that I'm going to detain him for the crime, I use a much "softer" approach.

Most of the time if a crime is serious enough that I'm going to get involved, the suspect has some sort of injury, exhaustion or behavior that allows me to ask, "Are you OK?"

Usually the suspect will say that he is OK and I'll follow up by asking, "What happened?" or encouraging him to sit down and rest a minute. By saying this I'm trying to project that I'm concerned about his well-being and don't want him to aggravate any injuries or problems he has. The reality is, while I may be concerned about his well being, I'm primarily interested in preventing him from fleeing until the police arrive.

In my experience, you'll find this "softer" approach to be useful in about half of the citizen arrest situations you come upon.

USE OF FORCE

When I worked as a loss prevention officer, I had to use force hundreds of times to apprehend thieves. However in the "real world" (not related to my job), while I've made "only" about half a dozen citizens arrest, the most force I've ever need to use was to gently hold onto the tail of the suspect's jacket from behind just in case the suspect decided to run. And while I held on firmly, I'm pretty sure the suspect didn't even know.

Reasonable.

MYTH: I've heard one so-called "expert" teaching you to use "whatever force is necessary". I get what he's trying to say, but it's *much* more accurate to say "use only a reasonable amount of force or preferably none at all".

The things I'm going to teach you about using force to make a citizen's arrest I base on those hundreds of apprehensions I made as a loss prevention officer when force was needed.

One of the first things you need to understand is to *avoid* using force if at all possible. Use "diplomacy" first to detain your suspect. In my experience, this is all it takes most of the time.

If you do decide you must use force, you must use the *least* amount of force necessary. Remember, you will absolutely be held accountable for your actions during the citizen's arrest!

My Rule of Thumb.

When you approach someone to make an arrest, I want you to presume that he knows everything you know... plus one more thing. I want you to presume that every punch, counter-punch, hold and joint lock you know he also knows. Plus presume he knows one more move you don't know! This presumption will help to keep you safe. It will help to keep you from being cocky.

This simple rule will help to prevent you from using force before it's necessary. Let me give you an example of when an inexperienced person might think force is necessary but it's not.

CASE STUDY: One time when I was dealing with a hostile street person, he began threatening me and spitting toward me. He was telling me all the diseases he had and that I should get away from him.

The interesting thing was he was spitting "toward" me and not really "at" or "on" me. What this means is he was trying too deter me from touching him so he could get away, but at the same time he wasn't truly ready (at that moment) to "attack" me. It's a subtle difference but it means he was still at the "threats stage" and not at the "use of force stage".

There was no reason, at that point, for me to use force when I could delay him using words (diplomacy) until the police arrived.

This is the type of thing that's only learned with *years* of experience, but I hope teaching it to you here allows you to take advantage of my experience and save yourself some grief.

WARNING: Using words rather than physical force does *not* relieve you of all liability.

It's important to remember that even without physically detaining someone, you can still be guilty of kidnapping or other crimes. While the laws vary from state to state, many states do *not* require physical force (or even moving the subject to a different location) in order to meet the elements of the felony crime of kidnapping.

This means if you've got the wrong person or made some other mistake during the citizen's arrest and the subject did not feel free to leave, you may find yourself being charged with a felony!

The key thing that will help you if you do have to physically detain someone is being able to articulate why you detained them and why you used the force you used.

In the heat of the moment you may be going on mostly instinct, but you still need to be able to explain what was your reasonable belief, your probable cause and why you used the amount of force you used. If you cannot explain those things you should not make an arrest.

"I can't breath."

What I'm about to share with you is based solely on my experience. I am not a doctor nor an attorney.

On the occasions when I have to use force to detain someone, the struggle almost always goes to the ground. On the ground it's not uncommon for me to be on top of someone or to have one or both of their arms in an awkward position while I attempt to restrain them. When this happens it's very common for the suspect to claim, "I can't breathe!"

This is a claim that you *must* take very, very seriously. Sometimes it's true. However in my experience most of the time it's a lie being told by the subject so he can obtain a tactical advantage to possibly hurt you so he can escape.

So when a suspect tells me he can't breathe, I take it very seriously but *without* revealing to him how seriously I take it. The only response he gets from me is I will calmly say, "I don't care."

Of course I *do* care and I care a great deal! First of all, my future and my well being is tied up in the suspect coming out of this OK. Second of all, I have no desire to hurt this person. All I want to do is detain him for the crime he committed and get the police there as quickly as possible.

The basic rule of thumb I follow is: If you can talk, you can breathe.

If the person truly could not breathe, they would be unable to tell me.

I've been involved in many arrest with the use of force when a police officer was there to assist me or I was assisting an officer, and in those circumstances when the suspect claims he can't breathe, every cop I've ever worked with will say to the suspect my exact rule of thumb, "If you can talk, you can breathe."

I'm not sure why police officers do this. When the person claims they can't breathe and it's a lie, the very act of them saying they can't breathe and is the "tell". And any poker player will explain, if you know a liar's "tell" you don't announce that you know it! As long as the person is complaining I know they can still breathe. But if you tell them the rule, then they can stop talking and you *can't* tell if they stopped breathing.

WARNING: It's important to remember that some people complain that they can't breathe when what they *really* mean is that they're having *difficulty* breathing. Either way, if someone tells you they can't breathe you must take it very, very seriously and act accordingly. You *will* be held accountable for what happens to that suspect.

My lawyer insist that I tell you again that I'm *not* a doctor and that you should check with a licensed physician if you have any questions about these things.

Avoiding a beating.

Most of the time when you're trying to make an arrest, the suspect doesn't want to truly "give you a beating". If he's going to hurt you at all, he only wants to hurt you enough so he can get away. This should be very comforting to you because most of the time if you find yourself getting the worst of it in a physical confrontation during a citizen's arrest, you can merely *let go* of the suspect and he will run away.

However if you find yourself in a situation where the person is being aggressive, coming for you and won't back down, this next tactic may help you.

CASE STUDY: One time in the course of my work I had an exceptionally aggressive confrontation with a street person. He came at me and I backed away, but he continued to come toward me. I retreated *literally* a block down the street, but he kept coming at me.

This guy was at least a foot taller than me, had a longer reach than me and was much stronger than me. I knew that if this confrontation turned physical I would end up in the hospital. My only thought was, "If I'm going to the hospital so is this guy."

When I determined it was inevitable that I would have to fight this guy, I moved off the sidewalk and into the middle of the busy street. He followed me and when I got halfway across the street I stopped and turned to face him.

Traffic stopped and I quickly had many witnesses to what was about to happen. At least I would have the consolation of knowing that I could easily prove he was the aggressor and that he threw the first punch. When he realized I was willing to stand and defend myself he had second thoughts. And when he realized there were plenty of legitimate witnesses around he decided to back off. He stormed off cursing.

This tactic of "taking it to the street" saved me from a pretty lopsided and severe being. And while I hope you never need to use this piece of advice, I hope my experience makes you better prepared just in case something like this happens to you.

SHOULD YOU USE A WEAPON?

I can say that with decades of experience in this field and hundreds of apprehensions under my belt, I have never carried a weapon.

This is not something I admit to most people. Those who know the life I lead just assume that I'm armed at all times. Nothing could be further from the truth.

I'm convinced that your brain is your best weapon and everything else is just a tool.

My view is that having a gun is like having a parachute. You could probably live 200 years and never need a parachute, but if you do need one, you really, really need one!

Of course this doesn't mean that I've never *apprehended* an armed suspect. I have. I've just never felt the need to carry a weapon myself.

When you make a citizen's arrest you have to consider that the suspect may have a weapon concealed on them. Definitely take this into consideration *before* you approach the suspect. If you feel you need to use a weapon against an unarmed suspect, chances are you should not be making the arrest.

This doesn't mean that it's illegal to use a weapon to make a citizen's arrest against an unarmed person, but I think it's unwise.

Let me give you a case study about a man who made a citizen's arrest using a gun against an unarmed person.

CASE STUDY: In one case, a motorist who said he saw a man in another car beating a woman forced the man out of the car at gunpoint and held him until the police arrived.

It appears that someone else (a "bystander") called the police to report an assault in progress. It appears that initially, the "good guy" making the citizen's arrest is called into the police as being the *bad guy* since the bystander hadn't seen the entire incident.

When officers arrived they found two men outside their vehicles in the middle of the roadway and one was pointing a gun at the other.

The man with the gun told police that he had seen the other man assaulting a female passenger. When both vehicles stopped, the man with the gun got out and pointed it at the other man and held him there for police.

Of course, traffic stopped in both directions until the police arrived. And while it didn't happen in this case, this did provided ample opportunity for an uninformed bystander to get *his* gun and "help" the suspect.

The man making the arrest with the gun had a permit to carry a concealed handgun. However, that's not legal grounds to use it during a citizen's arrest.

The police arrested the man who assaulted the woman. But the police also contacted the district attorney's office to determine if the man with the gun had violated a law.

Based on the *preliminary* investigation, no violation was apparent.

The man who made the arrest was fortunate that the people who decide whether or not to charge him with a crime seemed to feel that he acted reasonably. But it could have *easily* gone the other way.

What if the woman "protected" her boyfriend by saying there was no assault?

Why couldn't this "good guy" have just followed the car discreetly and called the police?

In my view this was really bad judgment and the citizen making the arrest got *very* lucky.

RESTRAINTS

Should you use physical restraints on the suspect?

Again, in my experience making citizen's arrests unrelated to any job I was working, I've *never* had to physically restrain the suspect. In one case I did firmly hold the tail of the suspect's jacket just in case the suspect tried to flee, but I'm pretty sure the suspect didn't even know I had a hold.

Even when I worked jobs where I was required to carry and use handcuffs, when I got home the cuffs came off my belt and I didn't wear them in my off time. I've never found it necessary to carry restraints of any kind in my off time.

If you think you need restraints (like handcuffs) to arrest a subject, you should seriously consider that you probably *shouldn't* make the arrest!

However if you do find yourself making an arrest that's serious enough that you believe it's reasonable to use restraints on the suspect, let me offer you some suggestions.

Handcuffs

You could carry handcuffs on yourself or keep them in your car "just in case you need them". But carrying them on yourself his bulky and uncomfortable. I highly recommend against that. Keeping them in your car will mean that 9 times out of 10 they will not be accessible to you if you do need them. Again I highly recommend against keeping handcuffs in your car.

Thumb Cuffs

Thumb cuffs are smaller and more lightweight than handcuffs and are much easier to carry in your pocket, but they are still heavier than you would want to carry and there is still no real reason to carry them on a daily basis. Plus they tend to cut into the thumbs leaving ghastly marks that will seem unreasonable to anyone viewing photos of them in the calm and safe environment of a courtroom. I highly recommend against carrying thumb cuffs.

Zip Ties

Large zip ties, which are available in any hardware store, may provide a lightweight alternative to handcuffs. Still, I can't think of a single legitimate reason to carry them daily on your person. And if you do have to use them, you may find yourself having to explain to the police, the prosecutor or a jury why you "just happen to have them on you".

It's easy for zip ties to cut into the suspect's wrist or to be tightened too tightly and this will leave marks on the suspect that will look severe and unreasonable in the photographs that are shown to a jury when the suspect sues you for excessive use of force. The suspect himself may cinch them down more tightly on his own wrist precisely so he can accuse you of excessive use of force!

I highly recommend against carrying or using zip ties "just in case".

Improvised Restraints

If you have handcuffs, thumb cuffs or zip ties on you it will appear as if you were overly eager to take someone into custody. Most people do not carry these tools with them and this means most people would not consider it "reasonable" that you have them or that you used them.

On the other hand, being able to "re-purpose" items most people routinely have on them and use those items as improvised restraints may seem much more reasonable to outsiders judging your actions.

Items that may be used in the unlikely case where you need to use "re-purposed" physical restraints are belts, shoelaces, bandanas, or maybe even a tee-shirt torn into strips of cloth suitable for tying.

Three Important Points

If you do find yourself needing to use a restraint to detain a suspect there are some key things to remember.

First of all, all restraints are temporary. Just because you've restrained the person does not mean they're going to stay restrained or that you can drop your guard. A restrained subject must be vigilantly watched at all times to prevent injury to himself, you or others.

Secondly, if you restrain a suspect you need to be prepared to *remove* the restraints. That means if you've tied the suspect using shoelaces and some crazy improvise knots, you've got to know how you're going to get them out of the restraints! If you can't easily untie the knot, you need to be prepared to cut the shoelaces to free the suspect. Of course introducing a knife into this situation may increase the level of danger.

And while I'd do not recommend carrying zip ties to restrain criminals, if you use a zip tie remember they have to be *cut* off and it's very difficult to do that safely with a knife.

The third thing you need to consider if you're going to restrain a suspect is that it is infinitely more difficult to restrain an unwilling person than you can possibly imagine. Even with handcuffs and proper training, experienced police officers find it difficult to restrain a criminal who's resisting.

WARNING: Finally, and most importantly, you need to remember the person you have restrained is in your custody and you're completely and 100% responsible for their well being.

If you've restrained them and they get hit by a car, that's your fault.

If you restrain them and they die because they were in a position where they couldn't breathe (positional asphyxiation), that's your fault. If you restrain a suspect and they loose feeling and one or more of their fingers, that's your fault. Can you see what I'm getting at here?

Not only can any one of the above listed bad things happen, there are a million more you and I could never think of! It is not a small thing to restrain a person. I would suggest that if you have to use a device to restrain them, you probably shouldn't be making the arrest.

PROTECTING YOUSELF EVEN MORE

As I explained earlier, video recordings have never given me any problems and have occasionally saved me a great deal a heartache by clearly showing my accounts of the event were accurate and my actions reasonable. Because of this I highly recommend you record your citizen's arrest if at all possible.

I believe it's best to record the arrest covertly if possible. You can do this by activating the video recorder on your cell phone and holding it at your side rather than pointing it directly at the person you're recording.

It's even better if someone reliable is nearby recording. This is because if *you're* recording, the suspect may take that as a disrespect or as an aggressive move and may escalate the amount of force he uses. Sometimes the issue quickly shifts from the crime he committed to the fact the you're recording him against his will.

My experience is if you're going to record openly, in other words the person knows you're recording them, it's best to begin recording before you approach the person rather than starting after you approached the person. First of all, starting the recorder distracts your attention from the suspect and increases the odds that you're going to be sucker punched. Secondly, in my experience, starting the recording *after* you've approached the subjects *instantly* outrage them.

Finally, don't forget that all 911 calls are recorded. So if you have called 911 and have the phone out as you engage the subject, while it might not be the best recording in the world, there will be somewhat of a recording of the things you and he say.

This can be extremely valuable if you can be heard saying calm and reasonable things such as, "Are you OK?"

Here's a tip that will help you anytime you need to call an ambulance for someone who doesn't want an ambulance called but still needs it. This is another one of my "magic phrases".

Simply say to the person, "Let's just call the squad. They can check you out and make sure you're OK. You can always refuse transport."

Many people are reluctant to have an ambulance called because they're concerned about going to the hospital. This can be for financial reasons, concerns about missing work or perhaps because they have a warrant out for their arrest. However the phrase, "You can always refuse transport." lets them know that they are in charge of what happens and calling an ambulance does not necessarily mean they're going to the hospital.

This is a helpful thing to remember if you're trying to use diplomacy to detain an injured suspect long enough for the police to arrive.

MIRANDA RIGHTS

Do you have to read the suspect his rights?

Miranda rights are the rights that protect us from the government in the United States. Law enforcement officers are required at certain times to "read a suspect his rights". Most of us are familiar with these rights from countless movies and TV shows. However, private citizens are not required to Mirandize their fellow citizens. And while I am not a lawyer and I'm not giving legal advice, I can tell you that I have never Mirandized any of the hundreds and hundreds of people I have apprehended. Not even on the countless occasions when I've had to handcuff the person.

CASE STUDY: One time a shoplifter did make the case that the charges should be dropped because I was acting as a "de facto agent of the state" rather that as an "agent of the merchant". There was a lengthy hearing on this and the judge listened patiently to both sides before ruling in my favor. However, he did point out that, while the defendant (the thief) was clearly wrong about this Miranda issue, if she had presented this to a jury rather than a judge, she might have "confused" the jury enough to convenience them that she was right.

My point here is, even though the law and the facts were (as the judge said) "clearly" on my side, it could have gone either way. Making an arrest is a risky thing.

While you don't have to read a person their rights, you do need to get the police on the scene as soon as possible.

CALLING THE POLICE

If you haven't *personally* called the police to the scene, make sure you designate a *specific* person to call the police.

HUGE TIP: If that person goes off to make the call because they don't have a phone with them, turn to a *second* person (after the first person/caller *leaves*) and say this magic phrase, "Call the police and verify that they're on the way." It's important to phrase it exactly like that because the second person can easily think to themselves that the first person has already called police and there's no need to make a call. But by using the phrase, "*verify* that they're on the way" means the second caller has a different responsibility than the first caller and is much more likely to fulfill that responsibility. All you really care about is that you know for certain that the police have been called.

While you're waiting for the police to arrive, and if it doesn't and aggravate the suspect, you have an opportunity to talk to him for a little bit. This is an excellent opportunity, especially if you're recording, to capture incriminating statements by the suspect.

While I've never found it necessary to *accuse* the suspect (and therefore avoided any arguments about his guilt), many times the suspect will be eager to justify what he did, trying to give an excuse or reason. The nice thing about this is that he's admitting to what he did and this can go a long way toward justifying your citizen's arrest.

WHAT THE SUSPECT SAYS

Listen to what the suspect says.. and maybe, just *maybe*... ask questions.

While it takes years of experience to do this well (and without aggravating your arrestee), here are example questions that are excellent traps if the subject answers them. I say "traps" because no matter how they answer the question, they're admitting to the crime.

1. "Did you know there was that much money?"

Any answer besides, "What money?" Or, "I don't know what you're talking about." means that the suspect knew there was some money before the incident or crime.

2. "She doesn't seem to care too much about the money but she does want her purse back. What'd you do with it?"

If the suspect tells you what he did with the purse, that's essentially an admission that he took it or at least had it in his possession. And that can go a long way towards establishing the elements of the crime.

3. "I can tell your a pretty decent guy. Why'd you do it? Did you need money for rent or groceries or something?"

This is a neat "trap" question because it allows the suspect to admit to the crime but also to show that he really had no choice.

That question is an example of a "presupposition" question. That means you're presenting it as a matter of fact that he did what he did (as if there's no question about it... and there shouldn't be if you're making an arrest), but you're allowing him to "save face" by demonstrating that in his shoes "anyone would have done it."

One of my favorite "trap" questions is an either/or question. For example...

"You're being a decent guy about this and I appreciate that. But I gotta' ask you about the knife. Were you going to cut someone or is it just for self defense."

Either way the suspect answers he's admitting that he carries the knife as a weapon. It's important to note, this isn't a question that tricks an innocent person. If the knife is *not* a weapon, an innocent person gives the legitimate reason for carrying the knife such as, "I use it for my job."

The things I'm teaching you in this book are things that I know from firsthand experience work for me. These little "rules of thumb" have helped to keep me safe both physically and legally.

If you decide to "break the rules" and wing it, trying to figure this out as you go along (or trying something new) you may find it leads you in a direction that hurts you more than it helps you.

In my experience, the only time to break the rules that I've developed based on my extensive personal experience, is when you know the rules cold! If you *really* know and understand the rules and *why* they're important, you may choose to break them.

Of course I'm not guaranteeing that these rules will keep you safe or out of trouble. I'm only saying they've worked well for me... so far.

Even so, there are times when I'll break my own rules. Here's an example...

WHEN TO BREAK THE "RULES"

As a general rule of thumb, when you take somebody into custody and they have car keys in their hand, you want to take possession of the car keys if reasonably possible. This prevents them from being used as a weapon against you and deprives the suspect of access to a vehicle for escape. However, this case study is a good example of when (and more importantly *why!*) I break my own rules.

CASE STUDY: One time when I made a citizen's arrest, it was of a drunk driver who had slammed into a lady's car. He fled in his car which was extensively damaged. Eventually he tried to hide the car and flee on foot, but he still had the car keys in his hand when I caught up to him.

Rather than taking possession of his car keys, I allowed him to keep them. This was a very conscious decision on my part.

I allowed him to keep the keys for two reasons. Number one: I knew his car was damaged badly enough that he couldn't drive it much further. Plus I felt confident that I could prevent him from getting back into the car if I had to. Number two (and *this* is the big reason), I wanted him to have *possession* of the keys when the police arrived. If he tried to claim he wasn't driving, it would be hard for him to explain why he had the car keys in his hand. Having the keys to the vehicle involved in the crime is a nice piece of evidence that he actually committed the crime! And as with all citizens arrest, a nice solid conviction goes a long way towards protecting me from accusations of false arrest.

Know the "rules" that help you make a citizen's arrest and only break them if you have a solid and articulable reason. You may choose to arrest someone differently than I teach you in this book, but you should understand what I'm teaching perfectly, then you can make an *informed* decision on if you want to try things your own way.

CAN YOU SEARCH THE SUSPECT?

Nope.

Searching the arrestee is a big deal. I have never searched someone I've arrested.

As a private citizen I would be comfortable seizing any weapons in the arrestee's possession, and maybe any evidence in plain view (if it could be readily taken away or destroyed). For example, I would have no problems picking up and keeping a purse the suspect threw down during a foot chase. But I would never "pat down" the suspect for drugs. There's a big difference to me between "seizing" a weapon the suspect already has out (in plain view) and "searching" the suspect for potential weapons or evidence.

In fact, I've *never* patted down an arrestee. Not even for a weapon! I figure if I am detaining him *properly*, he can't get to any weapon he may have. Some folks may argue this point, and I'll grant you they may have some valid reasons to take into consideration (and I consider those things as well!), but I've "been there and done that" and I've never needed to search a suspect. Not even for a weapon.

An exception?

In some states an "agent of the merchant" who arrests a suspect for theft, may request that he surrender the stolen property. If he refuses, the merchant may conduct a limited search of property in the immediate possession of the suspect, but not including any clothing worn by the suspect.

This is not the law in every state and even if it is legal where you are... Why would you do it? *Why conduct the search?*

If you aren't 100% sure the suspect has the stolen items on him, should you really be making the arrest? And if he *does* have the stolen items, let the police find them! It's so much more powerful when the police find a stolen purse stuffed in the guy's pants (it happens) than if they arrive and you've got the purse!

When the evidence is *on the suspect,* it makes it much harder for them to claim they didn't do the crime.

THE POLICE

If you've made a citizen's arrest, then your goal is to get your suspect safely into police custody as soon as possible. I don't mean *moving* the suspect or transporting the suspect to the police department. I mean getting the police to you and the suspect.

More on calling the police.

Once you've made the arrest and have custody the subject (or have tricked the subject into waiting for the police), you want to call the police and have them arrive expeditiously.

Remember, oftentimes you'll call the police *before* or even during the arrest, but if you haven't yet called the police, call them quickly after taking the suspect into custody.

It's important when you're speaking with the police operator that you remain calm, that you don't ramble, that you sound reasonable and you don't make any incriminating statements. It's important to remember all calls to 911 (and *many* calls to non-emergency police dispatch phone numbers) are recorded. Police detectives and the prosecutor's office may listen to your phone call later to determine if *you* committed a crime!

The suspect's defense attorney will also have access to the recording of this phone call. He or she may listen to it to discover if there's anything that can be turned to their client's advantage. Additionally, if you're sued in civil court, the plaintiff's attorney will listen to this phone call and see if there's anything he can use to his client's advantage.

When you're talking to the police dispatcher on the phone be concise.

Here's an example of the wrong way to report a crime:

"Um, yeah, I was pulling up to the drive through window at Qwick-Taco and I looked across the parking lot and I saw some guy pulling on a lady's purse. I wasn't sure what he was doing so I went over and talked to the lady and she said he tried to take her purse."

Here's an example of the exact same circumstance reported correctly:

"I'd like to report a purse snatching."

Notice the correct way is short and truthful, just the way I like all of my statements to the police to be.

After you make your initial, short statement to the police operator, she will usually began asking you questions. Some of those questions will include...

What is your location?
Does anyone need medical assistance?
Where's the suspect now?
Do you know who he is?
What does he look like?
What direction did he go?

I personally try to avoid saying anything to the police operator that sounds like I've taken the person into custody or made a citizen's arrest. In an ideal situation it should appear (and in reality frequently is) that the suspect is simply waiting with me of his own free will. (However, while I can't read the suspect's mind, most of the time I believe if I was *not* there, the suspect *would* flee.) But my authoritative presence "makes" the suspect stand-by and wait for the police to arrive.

Notice if that's the situation, the burden of proof falls upon the police or the suspect's attorney to prove beyond a reasonable doubt that I actually detained the suspect. This is very important to me because if they *can't* prove I detained the suspect, it makes it much more difficult for them to charge me with a crime or sue me in civil court. I certainly don't want to say anything on a recorded phone line that can be clearly taken as an admission that I detained a person. And I certainly want to avoid admitting that I used physical force to detain a person.

I absolutely will *not* lie, but I don't have to admit to anything either.

HUGE TIP: Because of the police operator's training and the questions she's asking you, she should understand that what you're calling about is essentially a *crime in progress*. In the unlikely event that she thinks the crime is over and an officer is simply needed to take a report, you need to make it clear that you need an officer right away.

WHEN THE POLICE ARRIVE

When the first officer arrives on the scene he may or may not know exactly what's going on. You may appear as "just another witness", the person who called the police ("the caller") or he might think you're the bad guy. Remember, at this point the officer is thinking primarily about his safety and the safety of the people on the scene. So when the police arrive make sure you do not have your hands in your pockets. Make sure your hands are in plain view. You *don't* have to hold your hands up unless the officer tells you to. Because of their extensive training and experience police officers automatically see whose hands are visible and empty and whose hands are hidden.

I usually let the police approach the scene and determine who they want to speak to first. If they don't go directly to someone I will tell them, "I'm the caller." This serves two purposes. First, it's much more likely that I am not the bad guy if I called the police. Secondly, they are looking for the suspect and if they know I'm the caller in gives me a little more credibility when I point out the suspect.

It's very common for the police to spend the first minute or two speaking with and dealing with the suspect. I never approach closer or interrupt the police during this time. They are gathering the information that they want. Anything the suspect says, the officers will remember and recorded in their report. When they need more information they will approach the person that they think can help them. Usually it's the victim they want to talk to next. After that, it's probably you they want to speak with... or they may not need you at all. And if the police don't need me, I certainly don't want to speak with them!

If you do speak with the police you want keep your statement concise and honest. Never lied to the police. You don't necessarily have to talk to them, but never lie to them!

When you speak with the police, speak with them like a normal citizen. Don't try to sound like a cop and don't imitate the slang or words you hear the police use in the movies. Do *not* refer to the bad guy as a "skell" or "perp". In fact, I don't even refer to him as a "suspect". Usually I just say "that guy" or use the pronoun "he". For example, "Then he hit her twice in the face."

I have never told the police that I've "made a citizen's arrest". And I've never used the words "detained" or "apprehended". The most I might say to the police about the "apprehension" might sound something like this:

"I walked towards the guy and I said, 'Hey, come here.' and he came back over and set down by the car here." (And, actually, I've never had to give *that* much detail to the police!)

Note that my statement to the police is accurate and true. I made a request and the guy complied.

Notice that I don't talk about asking to see his hands or asking if he has ID. I don't have to explain every little detail of what happen.

Aside from this book, I never even use the word "arrest". I'm only using it here for clarity. When I lecture or teach about these events later I always use the word "apprehension".

DO YOU MAKE A WRITTEN STATEMENT?

I've only once been asked to make a written statement by the police after a situation like this and I consented. It was after that felony burglary I witnessed as a K-9 patrol security officer, so strictly speaking it wasn't after a true "citizen's arrest". (I've never been asked by the police to write out a statement after making an actual citizen's arrest.) The statement I wrote after the burglary was something like this and it may prove to be a good model for you to follow…

"I arrived at the property and heard someone walking around on broken glass inside. Then I noticed that the front window was broken out. I observed the subject carrying computer equipment out of the building and hiding it in a nearby truck. He then departed northbound on foot through the park."

Obviously there were many, many more details I could have included about the crime that I had just witnessed. But my brief statement was accurate and established some of the elements of the crime such as the subject being in the building and removing property.

If more information is needed a police detective will contact you later.

Many attorneys might advise you *not* to make *any* statement to the police. Arguably this is in your best interest. However my experience speaking with them briefly and making only a short truthful statement has not gotten me in trouble. Not *yet* anyway.

I will say that about half the times that I've made a citizen's arrest *I've just walked away* after the police arrived. I don't mean that I sneaked away attempting not to get involved. It's simply been that the police arrived and quickly took charge of the situation, speaking with the suspect and the victim and needing no more information than that to do their job. When I can see that they clearly have no need for the guy who simply "fetched" the bad guy, there's no need for me to stick around.

On the other occasions I've been a valuable witness and I've been needed to make sure the bad guy gets charged with a crime.

MYTHS

There are two commonly given pieces of advice about making a citizen's arrest that, based on my experience, I don't necessarily agree with.

The "Include Everything" Myth

The first piece of advice I hear given is that you should "include everything" when you give a statement to the police. First of all, "everything" is seldom necessary. Things like whether you "ran" up to the suspect or "walked" up to the suspect don't necessarily make a difference. When I give a statement I simply say I "approached" the subject. Note I use the word "subject" or sometimes just "the guy" and *never* use the word "suspect". I want my statement to depict me as an innocent, average citizen off the street and not some "wannabe" who's looking for an opportunity to "play cop".

When I do give a written statement, I make sure to include any "elements of the crime" (although I never use that phrase). It's important to document the elements of the crime, such as the suspect's use of force or destruction of property.

The police and the prosecutor's office are experts on the elements of the crime in a way that you and I will never be. So, just as I don't write my statement to "play cop", I also don't write to "play lawyer" by trying to make my statement seem like a legal document.

The "Get It On Record ASAP" Myth

The second piece of advice I see commonly given for people making citizen's arrest is that it's "important to have everything on record as soon as possible." In my opinion, this is also not necessary.

As long as everything in your statement is true, you can always add to it later. If your statement doesn't contain the information the police or prosecutors need, it's their job to contact you and ask more questions. Again my thought is, if you give a statement at all, keep it short and truthful.

MORE ABOUT THE POLICE

One of the last questions the police will ask you on the scene is, "Are you willing to testify?"

I always answer yes, but I've never been called to testify in a case where I've made a citizen's arrest that was not related to a job I was being paid for. In other words, when I've just been out in the world living my life and I've made a citizen's arrest, I've never had to testify afterward. And there's a good reason for this...

In the half dozen or so citizen's arrest I've made, the cases have been so "open and shut" the bad guys *always* accept a plea bargain. Again, I don't get involved with every little crime I witness, so when I decide it's serious enough for me to make a citizen's arrest, there can be very little doubt by the police, prosecutors, judge or jury that the bad guy is 100% guilty.

On the scene of the citizen's arrest and even afterward, I've never been accused of doing anything inappropriate. However, when working as a loss prevention officer and making apprehensions on an almost daily basis, I have occasionally been accused of wrongdoing. Fortunately in every one of those cases, I've had access to recorded video which proves 100% my actions were legal an honorable.

However, when a false accusation is made it's important to get it documented as soon as possible so that the person who's lying is stuck of their original story. This is important because their initial statement (being a lie) will not mesh perfectly with the known facts. That means in order for the person to maintain their false accusation, they will have to change their story and sometimes change it repeatedly. This is good for you, as the truth teller, because it demonstrates that the liar's story has changed and your truthful statement has remained the same.

That doesn't mean you're in the clear, but it helps.

DO YOU NEED AN ATTORNEY?

I personally don't think it's a bad idea to get an attorney when you're dealing with the police or the prosecutor's office.

The police and the prosecutors are professionals and know a thousand times more about the law than you or I will ever know. If they decide (or even *think*) you may have broken the law, it's very likely that they will pursue charges against you. Having an attorney to protect your interests is vitally important at that time.

Although I have never retained an attorney after making a citizen's arrest, if I were to be approached afterward by a police detective or the prosecutor's office to give a follow-up statement, I might very well retain an attorney. And while I am not an attorney, I would advise you to retain one the first moment you even *think* you need one. Of course, most people don't realize they need a lawyer until they've dug themselves into a pretty deep legal hole!

LEGAL LIABILITY

Nothing in this book is legal advice. If you have legal questions contact a licensed attorney in your area.

Any decent defense attorney will tell you to *never* speak with the police or prosecutor's office without an experienced, licensed attorney representing you. I will concur that this is a good piece of advice.

The legal actions that take place *after* a citizen's arrest can drag on for a year or more, but frequently this is because of the defense attorney asking for continuances, motions of discovery and other legal maneuverings for the defendant who's looking for a way out.

If the police or prosecutor's office approach you for a second statement after you've made a citizen's arrest, that indicates to me there's some sort of problem. The case should have been open and shut enough to have been plead out. Either there's some question about the *suspect's* guilt or there's some question about the legality of what *you* did.

It's not uncommon for the police to approach someone seeming to ask for their help while *in reality* seeking for that person to make an incriminating statement. This is an excellent reason to have an attorney present if you give a statement to the police.

Remember when you make a citizen's arrest you open yourself up to accusations that you violated the law either civilly, criminally or both!

Criminally you may be charged with a variety of crimes such as false arrest, false imprisonment, kidnapping, disturbing the peace or any one of dozens of other criminal offenses. Civilly you may be sued by the suspect or *anyone* whose health or property was involved at the time of the citizen's arrest!

Depending on your state, the criminal charges can be filed as much as a year or more later depending on the crime they're accusing you of and the civil lawsuits can be filed two years or more after your citizen's arrest. These are significant and long-term consequences of making a citizen's arrest and they should make you *seriously* consider whether or not the arrest is worth it.

If you are sued in civil court by the person you arrested, you may find his attorney more dangerous than making the actual arrest was! Even if the person you arrested is *convicted* of the crime you arrested him a for, he can *still* sue you for a variety of things including any physical injuries he says he sustained during the arrest.

You also need to remember that when you take someone into custody ("arrest" them), their safety and well being is *your* responsibility and their attorney has a financial interest in suing you for *any* perceived wrong. That means a good attorney will actively be looking for the slightest reason to sue you in hopes that the lawsuit will be settled out of court and he or she can have a quick payday! And this can happen even if the defendant is found guilty of the crime.

COMMON MISTAKES

No crime occurred.

You cannot make a citizen's arrest if there was no crime.

Some states require that you actually witness the crime while other states only require that you have a "reasonable belief" that a crime (usually a felony) has occurred.

You have to ask yourself, "Would a reasonable and prudent person believe that a crime occurred?" This is what is known as "reasonable suspicion" and you need it before you can make an arrest.

If you cannot state clearly *why* you have a reason to believe a crime occurred, then you should not be making a citizen's arrest.

The crime is not a felony.

It is very important that you follow your state's laws regarding citizen's arrest and many states "require" that a citizen's arrest be made only for a felony.

It is true that some states have a very narrow exception to this felony requirement, but it clearly appears that the intent of any citizen's arrest law is that it is only to be used for serious crimes.

It's not hard to find examples in the news of a person attempting to make a citizen's arrest for a petty crime. The reason these examples make the news is because of the irony of the "good guy" being the one who goes to jail.

If you make a citizen's arrest for a non-felony, it is very likely you will be charged with a number of crimes including assault, false arrest and kidnapping.

Too much force is used.

It is very easy for an untrained and inexperienced person to use too much force when making a citizen's arrest. I believe this happens for two reasons.

First of all because the person making the arrest is full of adrenaline. This is a natural reaction to seeing a serious crime in progress and is a natural extension of the human "fight or flight" instinct. Secondly the person making the arrest feels self-righteous and justified to use "any means necessary" to catch the criminal who "deserves what he gets".

Neither one of those "reasons" is an excuse to use excessive force.

Even when using reasonable force, it's all too easy for outsiders to second guess your actions after the fact.

For example, if you're on the ground trying to detain a resisting suspect and he's trying to bite you, that may not be very obvious to outsiders. So any move you make to discourage him from biting you or to protect yourself will look (to the outside world) as if *you* are the aggressor. This is why it's not only important to use solely reasonable force, but also to be aware of what that reasonable force *looks like* to those outside the immediate danger zone.

Making an arrest at the wrong time.

A citizen's arrest must occur during or immediately after the felony crime.

It will not seem reasonable to anyone if you make the arrest a week, a day or even an hour after the crime.

If you see a person you know committed a crime and that crime has not occurred in the last few moments or minutes, it's obviously best just to call the police.

Use of restraints.

Using restraints to detain the suspect is rarely a good idea. I recognize that in some of the most extraordinary circumstances restraints may be necessary, however if the person is so dangerous that restraints are needed there's a good chance you should *not* be making the citizen's arrest.

You have to remember that this will all get sorted out six months or more from the time of the arrest. Your actions will be judged by people sitting in the safety of a comfortable courtroom. The suspect will be showered and neatly groomed. He'll be wearing a suit and all of his gang tattoos will be covered (hidden from the jury). The suspect will not look nearly as dangerous as he really is and your use of restraints will be judged very critically.

I highly discourage you from using restraints of any kind unless you sincerely believe someone's life is in danger… and then you better be able to convey that convincingly to those who will judge you and your actions.

Arresting the wrong person.

When a crime is in progress there's a great deal of uncertainty about what's happening. In combat this is referred to as "the fog of war."

Even professional, trained police officers can sometimes find it difficult when arriving on the scene of a crime to determine who's the victim and who's the criminal.

If you make a citizen's arrest based solely on what a "witnesses" or "victim" says to you, you may be making a very bad decision. Before you make an arrest you must have a very good reason to believe *that specific person* committed the crime. That reason is your "probable cause" to arrest this person.

If you're unable to explain in very clear language why you believe this person committed the crime, you should *not* be making the arrest.

CONCLUSION

Making a citizen's arrest is not a small thing. It is fraught with many dangers to yourself and to others both physically and legally. Making one wrong move or saying one wrong thing while arresting someone can cost you your health, your home and even your freedom.

I would highly encourage you never to make a citizen's arrest, but if you feel it's absolutely necessary, I hope the things you've learned in this book will give you the advantage you need to do it properly.

May God bless you and keep you.

APPENDIX OF STATE LAWS

Important Note: This list is only a *starting* place for your education. Laws change everyday and these laws may change at any time. Use the information here (including the "section numbers" of these laws) to help learn and understand the law in your area.

Furthermore, laws are shaped by "case precedent" (not listed here) meaning that court rulings on individual cases make a significant difference in how laws are interpreted.

It is solely *your* responsibility to know and follow the law in your area.

ARIZONA
13-3884
A private person may make an arrest:
(1.) When the person to be arrested has in his presence committed a misdemeanor amounting to a breach of the peace, or a felony.
(2.) When a felony has been in fact committed and he has reasonable ground to believe that the person to be arrested has committed it.

ARKANSAS
16-81-106. Authority to arrest

(d) A private person may make an arrest where he or she has reasonable grounds for believing that the person arrested has committed a felony.

CALIFORNIA
Rule 4.1
Authority To Arrest Without Warrant
(b) A private person may make an arrest where he has reasonable grounds for believing that the person arrested has committed a felony.

(c) An arrest shall not be deemed to have been made on insufficient cause hereunder solely on the ground that the officer or private citizen is unable to determine the particular offense which may have been committed.

A few California precedent setting cases:

People v. Garcia (1969) 274 Cal.App.2d 100, 105 ["When Edwards took defendant by the arm and told him he was going to call the police he effected a citizen's arrest"].

People v. Harris (1967) 256 Cal.App.2d 455, 459 ["[The citizen] did not state that defendant was under arrest, but such is not required where the accused is pursued immediately after the offense."].

Johanson v. DMV (1995) 36 Cal.App.4th 1209, 1217 ["[The citizen] witnessed the offense, summoned the officer, reported his observations, and pointed out the suspect. While [he] did not utter or write the 'magic words,' the substance of his actions constituted a valid citizens arrest."]

People v. Campbell (1972) 27 Cal.App.3d 849, 854 ["Nor under the circumstances of immediate pursuit was [the citizen] required to tell defendant that he was under arrest."]

People v. Sjosten (1968) 262 Cal.App.2d 539, 545 ["[I]t is well settled that were a party is apprehended in the commission of an offense or in fresh pursuit afterwards, failure to comply with section 841 does not invalidate the arrest."].

COLORADO
16-3-201
Arrest by a private person
A person who is not a peace officer may arrest another person when

any crime has been or is being committed by the arrested person in the presence of the person making the arrest.

CONNECTICUT
Sec. 54-170
Arrest without warrant
The arrest of a person may be lawfully made also by any peace officer or a private person, without a warrant, upon reasonable information that the accused stands charged in the courts of a state with a crime punishable by death or imprisonment for a term exceeding one year, but when so arrested the accused shall be taken before such a judge with all practicable speed and complaint shall be made against him under oath setting forth the ground for the arrest as in section 54-169; and thereafter his answer shall be heard as if he had been arrested on a warrant.

DELAWARE
§ 2514
Arrest without warrant.
The arrest of a person may be lawfully made by any peace officer or a private person, without a warrant, upon reasonable information that the accused stands charged in the courts of a state with a crime punishable by death or imprisonment for a term exceeding 1 year, but when so arrested the accused shall be taken before a judge or justice of the peace with all practicable speed and complaint shall be made against the accused under oath setting forth the ground for the arrest as in § 2513 of this title, and thereafter the accused's answer shall be heard as if the accused had been arrested on a warrant.

FLORIDA
941.14
Arrest without a warrant
The arrest of a person may be lawfully made also by any peace officer or a private person, without a warrant upon reasonable information that the accused stands charged in the courts of a state with a crime punishable by death or imprisonment for a term

exceeding 1 year, but when so arrested the accused must be taken before a judge with all practicable speed and complaint must be made against the accused under oath setting forth the ground for the arrest as in the preceding section; and thereafter his or her answer shall be heard as if the accused had been arrested on a warrant.

GEORGIA
O.C.G.A. 17-4-60 (2010)
§ 17-4-60
Grounds for arrest
A private person may arrest an offender if the offense is committed in his presence or within his immediate knowledge. If the offense is a felony and the offender is escaping or attempting to escape, a private person may arrest him upon reasonable and probable grounds of suspicion.

HAWAII
§832-14
Arrest without a warrant
The arrest of a person may be lawfully made also by any peace officer or a private person, without a warrant upon reasonable information that the accused stands charged in the courts of a state with a crime punishable by death or imprisonment for a term exceeding one year, but when so arrested the accused must be taken before a judge with all practicable speed and complaint must be made against the accused under oath setting forth the ground for the arrest as in section 832-13; and thereafter the accused's answer shall be heard as if the accused had been arrested on a warrant. [L 1941, c 99, §14; RL 1945, §10644; RL 1955, §250-14; HRS §713-14; am L 1970, c 188, §39; ren L 1972, c 9, pt of §1; gen ch 1985]

IDAHO
19-604
WHEN PRIVATE PERSON MAY ARREST
A private person may arrest another:

1. For a public offense committed or attempted in his presence.
2. When the person arrested has committed a felony, although not in his presence.
3. When a felony has been in fact committed, and he has reasonable cause for believing the person arrested to have committed it.

ILLINOIS
Sec. 107-3
Arrest by private person
Any person may arrest another when he has reasonable grounds to believe that an offense other than an ordinance violation is being committed.

INDIANA
IC 35-33-1-4
Any person
Sec. 4.
(a) Any person may arrest any other person if:
(1) the other person committed a felony in his presence;
(2) a felony has been committed and he has probable cause to believe that the other person has committed that felony; or
(3) a misdemeanor involving a breach of peace is being committed in his presence and the arrest is necessary to prevent the continuance of the breach of peace.
(b) A person making an arrest under this section shall, as soon as practical, notify a law enforcement officer and deliver custody of the person arrested to a law enforcement officer.
(c) The law enforcement officer may process the arrested person as if the officer had arrested him. The officer who receives or processes a person arrested by another under this section is not liable for false arrest or false imprisonment.

IOWA
804.9
Arrests by private persons

A private person may make an arrest:
1. For a public offense committed or attempted in the person's presence.
2. When a felony has been committed, and the person has reasonable ground for believing that the person to be arrested has committed it.

KANSAS

22-2403: Arrest by private person. A person who is not a law enforcement officer may arrest another person when:

(1) A felony has been or is being committed and the person making the arrest has probable cause to believe that the arrested person is guilty thereof; or

(2) any crime, other than a traffic infraction or a cigarette or tobacco infraction, has been or is being committed by the arrested person in the view of the person making the arrest.

KENTUCKY
431.005
(6) A private person may make an arrest when a felony has been committed in fact and he or she has probable cause to believe that the person being arrested has committed it.

LOUISIANA
Art. 214.
Arrest by private person; when lawful
A private person may make an arrest when the person arrested has committed a felony, whether in or out of his presence.

MAINE
§16.
Warrantless arrests by a private person
Except as otherwise specifically provided, a private person has the authority to arrest without a warrant: [2007, c. 173, §7 (AMD).]

1. Any person who the private person has probable cause to believe has committed or is committing:
   A. Murder; or [1977, c. 510, §25 (RPR).]
   B. Any Class A, Class B or Class C crime. [1975, c. 740, §22 (NEW).]
   [2007, c. 173, §7 (AMD) .]
2. Any person who, in fact, is committing in the private person's presence and in a public place any of the Class D or Class E crimes described in section 207; 209; 211; 254; 255-A; 501-A, subsection 1, paragraph B; 503; 751; 806; or 1002.
   A. [2007, c. 466, Pt. B, §12 (AFF); 2007, c. 466, Pt. B, §11 (RP).]
   [2007, c. 518, §5 (AMD) .]
3. For the purposes of subsection 2, in the presence has the same meaning given in section 15, subsection 2.
   [1975, c. 740, §22 (NEW) .]

MARYLAND
No specific statute

MASSACHUSSETS
No specific statute

MICHIGAN
764.16
Arrest by private person; situations
A private person may make an arrest—in the following situations:
(a) For a felony committed in the private person's presence.
(b) If the person to be arrested has committed a felony although not in the private person's presence.
(c) If the private person is summoned by a peace officer to assist the officer in making an arrest.
(d) If the private person is a merchant, an agent of a merchant, an employee of a merchant, or an independent contractor providing security for a merchant of a store and has reasonable cause to believe that the person to be arrested has violated section 356c or 356d of the Michigan penal code, Act No. 328 of the Public Acts of 1931,

being sections 750.356c and 750.356d of the Michigan Compiled Laws, in that store, regardless of whether the violation was committed in the presence of the private person.

MINNESOTA
629.37
WHEN PRIVATE PERSON MAY MAKE ARREST
A private person may arrest another:
(1) for a public offense committed or attempted in the arresting person's presence;
(2) when the person arrested has committed a felony, although not in the arresting person's presence; or
(3) when a felony has in fact been committed, and the arresting person has reasonable cause for believing the person arrested to have committed it.

MISSISSIPPI
§ 99-3-7
When arrests may be made without warrant
(1) An officer or private person may arrest any person without warrant, for an indictable offense committed, or a breach of the peace threatened or attempted in his presence; or when a person has committed a felony, though not in his presence; or when a felony has been committed, and he has reasonable ground to suspect and believe the person proposed to be arrested to have committed it; or on a charge, made upon reasonable cause, of the commission of a felony by the party proposed to be arrested. And in all cases of arrests without warrant, the person making such arrest must inform the accused of the object and cause of the arrest, except when he is in the actual commission of the offense, or is arrested on pursuit.

MISSOURI
No specific statute

MONTANA
46-6-502
Arrest by private person

(1) A private person may arrest another when there is probable cause to believe that the person is committing or has committed an offense and the existing circumstances require the person's immediate arrest. The private person may use reasonable force to detain the arrested person.
(2) A private person making an arrest shall immediately notify the nearest available law enforcement agency or peace officer and give custody of the person arrested to the officer or agency.

NEBRASKA
29-402
Any person not an officer may, without warrant, arrest any person, if a petit larceny or a felony has been committed, and there is reasonable ground to believe the person arrested guilty of such offense, and may detain him until a legal warrant can be obtained.

NEVADA
NRS 171.126
Arrest by private person

A private person may arrest another:
1. For a public offense committed or attempted in the person's presence.
2. When the person arrested has committed a felony, although not in the person's presence.
3. When a felony has been in fact committed, and the private person has reasonable cause for believing the person arrested to have committed it.

NEW HAMPSHIRE
No specific statute

NEW JERSEY
2C:13-3. False imprisonment
 A person commits a disorderly persons offense if he knowingly restrains another unlawfully so as to interfere substantially with his liberty.

And...

3.20 FALSE IMPRISONMENT (FALSE ARREST) (Approved 6/89)

NEW MEXICO
Section 31-4-14
Arrest without a warrant
The arrest of a person may be lawfully made also by any peace officer or a private person without a warrant upon reasonable information that the accused stands charged in the courts of a state with a crime punishable by death or imprisonment for a term exceeding one year, but when so arrested the accused must be taken before a judge or magistrate with all practicable speed and complaint must be made against him under oath setting forth the ground for the arrest as in the preceding section [31-4-13 NMSA 1978]; and thereafter his answer shall be heard as if he had been arrested on a warrant.

NEW YORK
N.Y. CPL. LAW § 140.30
Arrest without a warrant; by any person; when and where authorized
1. Subject to the provisions of subdivision two, any person may arrest another person
> (a) for a felony when the latter has in fact committed such felony, and (b) for any offense when the latter has in fact committed such offense in his presence.

2. Such an arrest, if for a felony, may be made anywhere in the state. If the arrest is for an offense other than a felony, it may be made only in the county in which such offense was committed.

NORTH CAROLINA
§ 15A-404. Detention of offenders by private persons.
(a) No Arrest; Detention Permitted. – No private person may arrest another person except as provided in G.S. 15A-405. A private person

may detain another person as provided in this section.

(b) When Detention Permitted. – A private person may detain another person when he has probable cause to believe that the person detained has committed in his presence:

(1) A felony,

(2) A breach of the peace,

(3) A crime involving physical injury to another person, or

(4) A crime involving theft or destruction of property.

(c) Manner of Detention. – The detention must be in a reasonable manner considering the offense involved and the circumstances of the detention.

(d) Period of Detention. – The detention may be no longer than the time required for the earliest of the following:

(1) The determination that no offense has been committed.

(2) Surrender of the person detained to a law-enforcement officer as provided in subsection (e).

(e) Surrender to Officer. – A private person who detains another must immediately notify a law-enforcement officer and must, unless he releases the person earlier as required by subsection (d), surrender the person detained to the law-enforcement officer. (1973, c. 1286, s. 1.)

NORTH DAKOTA
29-06-20

When private person may arrest

A private person may arrest another:

1. For a public offense committed or attempted in the arresting person's presence.

2. When the person arrested has committed a felony, although not in the arresting person's presence.

3. When a felony has been in fact committed, and the arresting person has reasonable grounds to believe the person arrested to have committed it

OHIO
2935.04

When any person may arrest

When a felony has been committed, or there is reasonable ground to believe that a felony has been committed, any person without a warrant may arrest another whom he has reasonable cause to believe is guilty of the offense, and detain him until a warrant can be obtained.

OKLAHOMA
Section 202
Authority of Private Person to Arrest Another
A private person may arrest another:
1. For a public offense committed or attempted in his presence.
2. When the person arrested has committed a felony although not in his presence.
3. When a felony has been in fact committed, and he has reasonable cause for believing the person arrested to have committed it.

OREGON
133.805
(1) A private person may arrest another person for any crime committed in the presence of the private person if the private person has probable cause to believe the arrested person committed the crime. A private person making such an arrest shall, without unnecessary delay, take the arrested person before a magistrate or deliver the arrested person to a peace officer.

(2) In order to make the arrest a private person may use physical force as is justifiable under ORS 161.255. [1973 c.836 §74]

PENNSYLVANNIA
No specific statute

RHODE ISLAND
§ 12-9-17
Arrest without warrant
The arrest of a person may also be lawfully made by any peace officer or a private person without a warrant, upon reasonable

information that the accused stands charged in the courts of a state with a crime punishable by death or imprisonment for a term exceeding one year, but when so arrested, the accused must be taken before a judge with all practicable speed, and complaint must be made against him or her under oath, setting forth the ground for the arrest as in § 12-9-16; and thereafter after that his or her answer shall be heard as if he or she had been arrested on a warrant.

SOUTH CAROLINA
SECTION 17-13-10
Circumstances when any person may arrest a felon or thief
Upon
(a) view of a felony committed,
(b) certain information that a felony has been committed or
(c) view of a larceny committed, any person may arrest the felon or thief and take him to a judge or magistrate, to be dealt with according to law.

SOUTH DAKOTA
§23A-3-3
Citizen's arrest
Any person may arrest another:
(1) For a public offense, other than a petty offense, committed or attempted in his presence; or
(2) For a felony which has been in fact committed although not in his presence, if he has probable cause to believe the person to be arrested committed it.

TENNESSEE
40-7-109
Arrest by private person Grounds
(a) A private person may arrest another:
    (1) For a public offense committed in the arresting person's presence;
    (2) When the person arrested has committed a felony, although not in the arresting person's presence; or
    (3) When a felony has been committed, and the arresting

person has reasonable cause to believe that the person arrested committed the felony.

(b) A private person who makes an arrest of another pursuant to the provisions of §§ 40-7-109 40-7-115 shall receive no arrest fee or compensation for the arrest.

TEXAS
CHAPTER 14 Arrest without Warrant
Art. 14.01 Offense within view
(a) A peace officer or any other person, may, without a warrant, arrest an offender when the offense is committed in his presence or within his view, if the offense is one classed as a felony or as an offense against the public peace.
(b) A peace officer may arrest an offender without a warrant for any offense committed in his presence or within his view.

UTAH
77-7-3
By private persons
A private person may arrest another:
(1) For a public offense committed or attempted in his presence; or
(2) When a felony has been committed and he has reasonable cause to believe the person arrested has committed it.

VERMONT
No specific statute

VIRGINIA
§ 19.2-100.
Arrest without warrant.
The arrest of a person may be lawfully made also by any peace officer or private person without a warrant upon reasonable information that the accused stands charged in the courts of a state with a crime punishable by death or imprisonment for a term exceeding one year. But when so arrested the accused shall be taken before a judge, magistrate or other officer authorized to issue criminal warrants in this Commonwealth with all practicable speed

and complaint made against him under oath setting forth the ground for the arrest as in the preceding section; and thereafter his answer shall be heard as if he had been arrested on a warrant.

WASHINGTON
No specific statute

WEST VIRGINIA
No specific statute

WISCONSIN
No specific statute

WYOMING
7-8-101
Arrest by private person
(a) A person who is not a peace officer may arrest another for:
    (i) A felony committed in his presence;
    (ii) A felony which has been committed, even though not in his presence, if he has probable cause to believe the person to be arrested committed it; or
    (iii) The following misdemeanors committed in his presence:
        (A) A misdemeanor theft offense defined by W.S. 6-3-402; or
        (B) A misdemeanor property destruction offense defined by W.S. 6-3-201.

ALSO BY LARRY KAYE

51 Dirty Tricks Bad Guys Really Hate:
Sneaky Tactics used by Police, Private Investigators and Bounty Hunters

This book reveals...

- How a dirty cop can beat the daylights out of a completely compliant subject, on video, and get away with it every time!

- The social media Dirty Trick Al-Queda used to blow up 4 Top Secret U.S. helicopters!

- WARNING: Don't even think about using any of the Dirty Tricks in the "Off Limits" chapter!

- The one Dirty Trick thieves hate even more than getting caught!

- The "Freakishly Effective" Dirty Trick to catch underage drinkers in a bar. (This is one I almost didn't include!)

- The Dirty Trick cops use to shut down a Private Investigator's surveillance in 30 seconds or less.

- Section on Little Known Sources of Info (If you're a real-world P.I. you better learn these!)

- The "Particularly Devastating" trick to catch a liar. (That's what the U.S Government said in a previously classified report!)

- The Post Card Dirty Trick. (This is so powerful it's one of my all-time favorites!)

- And Much, Much More!

Learn more at: **www.51DirtyTricks.com**

The Investigator's Ultimate Guide to Missing Persons and Fugitives.

- See why needing a friendly cop to feed you information is 100% bogus. (In fact you'll learn why cops hire PI's!)

- The "Big Daddy" of Skip Tracing Secrets. How to find the SSN of just about anyone! This is so easy it's scary, once you know the secret!

- How to get paid BEFORE you find the person you're looking for!

- The "dirty little secret" that most Private Detectives do not want you to know.

- A very simple tactic that makes potential clients choose you rather than another P.I. This tactic turns leads into paying cases! (This secret can be explained in three short words.)

- How to cover your butt with a strong Investigative Contract. (You get the exact contract used in the real world!)

- And much, much more!

Available at: **www.BeaPI.com**

The Investigator's Ultimate Guide to Surveillance.

- What lane you should REALLY be in when following someone on the highway.

- What to do when you lose the subject.

- Actual case video examples.

- How to crack a PO box or Private Mail Box with a broom. (Use this Dirty Trick so you don't have to watch a PO Box 24/7/365!)

- Two magic words that almost turn off a cop's brain and make him walk away from you when you're on surveillance – without making him your enemy!

- Why shaving cream should be part of your pre-surveillance routine (Hint: It has nothing to do with shaving).

- Should you be armed when working surveillance? (This controversial answer may surprise you!)

- Two ways to get the real-world practice you need to build your skills.

- REVEALED: Marketing Secrets so powerful you'll "legally steal" cases from your competition. (Including the Three Magic Words that turn a price shopper into a paying client).

- And much, much more!

Available at: **www.ShadowAnyone.com**

The Investigator's Ultimate Guide to Process Serving.

- How to compete for business without compromising on price.

- A very simple tactic that will get you your first case with just about any law firm.

- The dirty little secret of "Going Nuclear" on someone refusing to be served.

- Larry's "<u>Never Fail</u>" method for even the most die-hard refuser.

- How to handle a pretext gone bad. (Get this wrong and you – or someone near you – is going to get a beating.)

- Why a classic process server trick may fail you and what to do about it.

- The absolutely wrong thing to say to refusers (and most process servers say it).

- When you should <u>NEVER</u> I.D. yourself as an Officer of the Court.

- The secret to stopping the "Snowball Effect"

- The Extreme Measures Section. When you need to get brutal, go right to this section.

- And much, much more!

Available at: www.ShadowAnyone.com/ps

Made in the USA
San Bernardino, CA
03 March 2020